IM/MIGRANT
NAIROBI

Published and distributed by
Im/migrant Nairobi

✉ immigrantnairobi@gmail.com
 www.instagram.com/immigrantnairobi
 www.twitter.com/immigrantnbo

Edited and produced by Sandra Zhao & April Dodd

Photography by Sandra Zhao, Roopa Gogineni,
Pedro Ramirez Paz and Tomas Benito
Food styling by Sandra Zhao and Roopa Gogineni
Concept & Art Direction by Barbara Muriungi
Book Design by Barbara Muriungi

©2016 Im/migrant Nairobi
ISBN 978-0-692-82116-9

All rights reserved. No part of this publication may be reproduced, stored in retrieval systems or transmitted in any form or by any means, electronic, mechanical, photocopying, recording or any information storage, without written permission from the respective copyright owners.

Produced, edited and designed in Nairobi, Kenya
Printed and bound in the USA

IM/MIGRANT NAIROBI

~ A COOKBOOK ~

RECIPES & STORIES FROM NAIROBI'S
IMMIGRANT RESTAURANTS

by
SANDRA ZHAO & APRIL DODD

photography by
SANDRA ZHAO, ROOPA GOGINENI, PEDRO RAMIREZ PAZ and TOMAS BENITO

Foreword

Today, Nairobi is a city of approximately 3.5 million people. A hundred years ago, it was a tiny train depot, established because of its convenient location between Mombasa, Kenya's major coastal port, and Kampala, the capital of Uganda. Nairobi's rapid expansion can be attributed to factors ranging from geographic to geopolitical, but the city's growth ultimately comes down to the individuals who chose to leave what they knew and take their chances in a new place. This migration happened internally, bringing people from all of Kenya's many ethnic communities to the young capital city. But Nairobi also became a magnet for immigrants from all over the world, and their stories reflect phenomena that have been shaping Nairobi—and so many other cities—over the last century.

Hundreds of books can and have been written on the cultural exchanges created by human migration. But in the cookbook genre, little attention has been given to the resulting culinary richness of African cities. Perhaps, we realized, this is not a result of antipathy but unfamiliarity: people uninitiated to Kenya simply may not expect that its capital would offer cuisines ranging from Brazilian to Thai. They certainly wouldn't anticipate the level of creativity that this city's chefs have had to reach in order to make unfamiliar tastes interesting for a Kenyan audience. And it's only in talking with the restaurateurs themselves that you see how hard they work to create spaces that feel like home for their respective diasporas—while also making anyone and everyone feel welcome.

So we decided to write a book that, we hope, conveys some of the creativity, bravery, and culinary insight of Nairobi's immigrant restaurateurs. They have kindly shared their stories, which you'll find scattered throughout the book in chronological order, starting in 1977 and continuing right up to 2016. They also gave us some of their most beloved recipes, which we've tested to make sure they're approachable for the home cook.

We hope that you enjoy reading about these amazing people and trying out their recipes yourself. We also hope that this book will inspire reflection on assumptions about cities in Africa and throughout the so-called global south. Human migration is changing the face of the world over, and open-minded exchange is enriching for all involved—especially when it happens around a shared table.

April & Sandra

Using This Book

All volume measurements in this cookbook are given first in U.S units, followed in parentheses by metric measurements. For ease of readability, length measures are given only in inches, which can be easily converted to centimeters by multiplying by 2.5 or referring to the ruler at right (or left, TBD).

When measuring dry ingredients by volume, always overfill your cups or spoons and then level the top with the back of a knife or your finger. When measuring liquids by volume, fill the cup or spoon completely (or use a liquid measure).

It's always a good idea to first measure dry ingredients and then proceed to wet ones, as this lets you reuse your measuring utensils without having to wash and dry them. When measuring sticky things (like peanut butter, honey, or tahini), first brush the inside of the cup or spoon with a little neutral oil, which helps the ingredient in question to come out easily.

Always feel free to multiply and divide recipes to make them suitable for larger or smaller groups. When increasing quantities, be cautious about upping the quantity of hot peppers, chili powder, and dry spices. A good rule of thumb is to increase these ingredients by half when doubling, then adjust to taste just before serving.

When bringing water or stock to a boil, cover the pot with a lid to trap heat and save energy. When heating oil, resist the urge to speed the process by covering it: condensation will gather on the underside of the lid and drip into the oil, causing it to spatter.

We have done our best to make the language in this book universal, though we default to the U.S standard when there are multiple options. Some notable examples: we use baking soda, which is called bicarbonate of soda in some areas; cornstarch, which also goes by cornflour; and cilantro, which some would call fresh coriander (or, in Swahili, dhania).

Nairobi-based folks may notice that some beloved restaurants are missing from this book. In some cases, our request to publish recipes for all to see proved too big an ask, and we completely respect their decision to keep their secret sauces secret. In order to reflect the culinary diversity of our city, though, we have included some recipes that are inspired by a specific restaurant. These few recipes are our own creations, created by trial and error to approximate the flavors we love.

Contents

4	Foreword
5	Using this book
9	Appetizers
49	Soups & salads
81	Sides
99	Vegetable Mains
131	Meat Mains
191	Fish & Seafood Mains
219	Desserts
241	Drinks
258	Reference Charts
259	Index
262	Acknowledgements

Appetizers

10	BABA GHANOUSH	Cedars
12	PICKLES	Cedars
14	LABNEH	Cedars
18	TOMATO & BRIE SAMOSAS	Purdy Arms
20	PESTO	Osteria
22	MOZZARELLA	Osteria
26	FRIED PORK DUMPLINGS	Cai Lan Chao Shi
28	SEAFOOD WONTONS	Cai Lan Chao Shi
30	FUUL MEDAMES	D'Afric
32	SALATA ASWAT	D'Afric
36	TEMPURA PRAWNS	Furusato
38	CHILLY GARLIC MUSHROOM	Open House
40	CHICKEN WINGS	Tin Tin
44	BRAISED PORK BELLY	Cheka
46	FRIED OCTOPUS	Cheka

~~~ CEDARS ~~~

BABA GHANOUSH

SERVES

8, as an appetizer

A wonderful alternative to the ever-present hummus, baba ghanoush is a versatile spread that replaces chickpeas with roasted eggplant. Don't be afraid to really let the skins of the eggplants blacken when you roast them: this is the one time that you should want that burnt smell.

TIME

Total Time: 45 minutes
Active Time: 15 minutes

INGREDIENTS

3 medium eggplants
1 teaspoon salt, plus more to taste
2 teaspoons lemon juice, plus more to taste
¾ cup (200 grams) tahini paste
1 cup + 2 tablespoons (250 grams) plain yogurt
¼ cup (25 grams) chopped fresh parsley
Olive oil and paprika, to garnish
4 tablespoons ghee or unsalted butter

PREPARATION

1. Roast the eggplants. You can do this in one of two ways:
- In the oven: turn your broiler to high heat. Place the whole eggplants on a baking sheet just under the broiler. Roast the eggplants, turning every 3-5 minutes, until the skin is black on all sides, about 15 minutes total.
- Over a gas stove: turn the gas on high on three burners. Place the eggplants directly over the open flame. Turn them every 2-3 minutes, until the skin is charred all over.

2. Peel the eggplants: Place the roasted eggplants in a bowl and cover with a lid or cloth. (Trapping the moisture in this way makes it easier to peel the skins away from the eggplants.) Once the eggplants are cool, cut off the stems and peel off the blackened skins. Discard the skins and roughly chop the meat of the eggplant.

3. Blend: Using a food processor or a blender, purée the eggplant with the salt, lemon juice, tahini, and yogurt until smooth. If you don't have a food processor or blender, you can use a fork to smash the eggplant with the other ingredients.

4. Season: Add the chopped parsley and stir. Taste; add salt and additional lemon juice to your liking.

5. Serve: Serve with a drizzle of olive oil and a sprinkle of paprika, alongside bread or pita chips.

~~~ CEDARS ~~~

PICKLES

 SERVES
Many, as an appetizer or snack

These are the world's simplest pickles: simply chop up a handful of vegetables, toss them in a vinegar brine, and wait. There's no boiling and no need for refrigeration as they soak. Fair warning, though: the beets will turn everything pink. If you prefer to keep your turnips white and your cucumbers green, then soak the beets separately.

 TIME
Total Time: 3-6 days
Active Time: 20 minutes

 PREPARATION

1. Prepare the vegetables: Cut the beets, turnips, and cucumbers into slices about 1/4 inch thick. You can leave them as dics or cut them into halves or eighths, depending on the size you'd like your pickles to have.

2. Make the brine: Place the crushed garlic and sliced vegetables in a non-reactive container with at least a 2 liter capacity. Pour the water and vinegar over. If the liquid doesn't cover the vegetables, add more brine until everything is submerged.

3. Season: Add the salt and stir.

4. Wait: Cover the container and let it sit in a cool place for 3 days. After 3 days, taste the pickles; if they are not yet to your liking, let them sit for another day or two. We like them best after six full days of soaking.

5. Serve: Enjoy alongside a platter of pita bread and baba ghanoush.

 INGREDIENTS
3 large beets, peeled
2 turnips, peeled
2 cucumbers
1 head garlic, peeled and crushed
3 cups (720 mL) water
2 cups (480 mL) white or apple cider vinegar
4 tablespoons kosher salt

NOTES
Be sure to remove and discard the ends of the cucumbers, as they contain enzymes that can make pickles mushy.

~ CEDARS ~

LABNEH

YIELD
4 cups labneh
(and 4 cups whey)

TIME
Total Time: 16 - 36 hours
Active Time: 20 minutes

SPECIAL TOOLS
Cheesecloth

INGREDIENTS
8 cups (2 litres) whole milk
1/2 cup (110 grams) full-fat yogurt, with live cultures
1/4 teaspoon salt
Olive oil and paprika, to garnish

Step one for Cedars' labneh is making a big batch of homemade yogurt. Step two is straining that yogurt until it's very thick and extra creamy.

PREPARATION

1. Heat the milk: Over medium heat, bring the milk to a near boil (about 200F/93C), stirring it occasionally to ensure it doesn't scorch on the bottom of the pan. Then, turn off the heat and allow the milk to cool to body temperature (98F/37C).

2. Temper the yogurt: Place your live culture yogurt in a small bowl. Slowly stir in one cup of the warm milk, whisking thoroughly to combine. Then, whisk the yogurt & milk mixture back into the big pot of milk.

3. Let the milk culture: Place the pot of cultured milk in a warm place. This can be in a pre-warmed oven with the heat turned off, or set into a larger bowl filled with warm water. In either case, be sure to cover the pot with a lid or a clean kitchen towel. Wait for at least four hours. If you like your yogurt extra tangy, you can let the milk culture for 12-16 hours.

4. Strain: After 4+ hours, you should have a pot of nicely set yogurt. Place a piece of cheesecloth in a mesh strainer and pour the yogurt into it. Then, tie the ends of the cheesecloth together and hang the bundle up over a bowl for at least 4 hours.

5. Serve: After 4+ hours, the labneh should be very thick. Give the cheesecloth bundle a final squeeze to remove excess moisture, then transfer the labneh to a bowl and gently stir in the salt. Drizzle it with olive oil and sprinkle with paprika, if desired.

NOTES

If you're not sure whether your yogurt is live or not, look for the words *Lactobacillus bulgaricus,* S*treptococcus thermophilus,* and/or *acidophilus* on the container. Or, your yogurt may say "contains live and active cultures."

Plan to lose about 1/2 of the volume of your yogurt in the straining process. So, if you'd like to end up with 2 cups of labneh, start with 4 cups of yogurt, and so on. The liquid that strains out of the labneh (the whey) can be discarded or used in place of buttermilk in future recipes.

"In those days nothing could stop me."

Christian, Jardin du Paris

Jardin du Paris

Our story about immigrant restaurant owners in Nairobi begins with Christian Caldara, the founder of the now closed Jardin du Paris. Like many who came after him, his love story with Nairobi transpired in part by luck and very much by accident.

Christian's story starts in Morocco in the 1960s, where as an adventurous teenager, he met an American in Casablanca who owned curio shops in the US and traveled the world looking for treasure. While transiting through London on his way home to Paris, he was riding the Tube one day when the doors opened at Piccadilly Station and he found himself face to face with the American from Morocco. Christian joined him at a bed and breakfast where the American regaled him with stories of Kenya, a place that felt unimaginably far away. Kenya remained in the back of Christian's mind as he finished culinary school in France and moved to Scotland to work as a cook. Unable to resist the pull of adventure, Christian decided to leave his job and, with an introduction from the American to an Indian Kenyan tour guide, he was soon on his way to Nairobi with a one-way ticket and eighty pounds in his pocket. It was 1978, and he was eighteen years old.

Christian started out giving French lessons to the children of Indian Kenyans and cooking for private parties. As his network and reputation grew, he soon landed a job as the chef for the newly established United Nations Environment Program (UNEP). In 1977, the French Embassy asked him to manage their cafeteria, which became his Montmarte-inspired bistro, Jardin du Paris. He eventually closed that restaurant and joined forces with a Nairobi legend, the French restaurateur Alan Bobbe, to run his eponymous restaurant, eventually being named Alan's heir and inheriting the business and brand when he died. A few years ago he sold the restaurant and left the industry for good.

The son of a chef and grandson of confectioners, Christian grew up around food and it's clear that even now, after more than forty years in the restaurant industry, he still has a great love for cuisine. When I asked him if he ever had difficulty getting ingredients back when he was getting started, he brushed off the question, saying that there was always a shortage of something, but "in those days nothing could stop me." If there wasn't butter, he'd buy cream and make it himself. If he couldn't get olive oil, he'd buy it at the pharmacy, where it was sold as a laxative. He found English home cooks who were making their own cheddar, feta, chevre and Camembert at home. If nothing else worked, he'd get seeds and plant lettuces, herbs, cardoons and artichokes himself.

When I met him, he was wearing his uniform of khaki pants, a safari vest covered in pockets, and a safari hat (we were indoors). We sat in the newest iteration of his restaurant at the Alliance Française, now in its third life, where he holds court a few times a week, catching up with old friends and enjoying the bustle of downtown Nairobi.

Since moving to Nairobi, Christian has returned to France only three times and became a Kenyan citizen in 1996. Not content to enjoy retirement, Christian is now reinventing himself as an adventurer. Having established his legacy in Nairobi as a French chef, he is now constructing a safari lodge a few hours south of Nairobi. His dream is to host archaeologists and anthropologists and perhaps make discoveries of his own someday. Once an adventurer, always an adventurer.

TOMATO & BRIE SAMOSAS

 SERVES
4-6, as an appetizer

The Purdy Arms deep fries their samosas, but the home cook can simply fry them in a small amount of oil. For an even healthier samosa, it's also possible to bake them: just preheat the oven to 400F (200C) and bake until the samosas are golden brown all over, 10-15 minutes.

 TIME
Total Time: 15 minutes
Active Time: 15 minutes

 INGREDIENTS
1/4 round of brie (about 40 grams), chopped into small pieces
1 medium yellow onion, minced
8-10 sundried tomatoes, finely chopped
Pinch of salt
12 samosa wrappers
6 tablespoons oil

 PREPARATION

1. Make the filling: Combine the chopped brie, onion, and sundried tomatoes in a medium bowl. Add a pinch of salt.

2. Fold the samosas: Lay the samosa wrappers out on a clean counter. Brush them very lightly with water to keep them from drying out. Place about 1 tablespoon of filling at the top of each wrapper. Fold the top-right corner downward and to the left to form a right triangle; then, fold the triangle directly downward. Continue folding across and down until the filling is completely enclosed, then brush the bottom edge of the samosa wrapper with water and press to seal.

3. Cook: Heat 3 tablespoons of oil over medium heat in a large, heavy pan. Place half the samosas in the pan and cook for 2-3 minutes, until the bottom side is nicely browned. Flip the samosas over and cook 2-3 minutes on the other side. Place the cooked samosas on a paper towel-lined plate while you cook the second batch.

4. Serve: Serve the samosas as an appetizer, perhaps with a little pesto (see page 20).

NOTES

You can use pre-cut samosa wrappers for these samosas; they're easy to find in the frozen foods section of the grocery. Just remember to take them out of the freezer at least 12 hours before you intend to use them. If you'd like a larger samosa, you can also buy rolls of puff pastry dough and cut them into long rectangles, increasing the amount of filling in proportion to the size of the wrapper.

~~~ OSTERIA ~~~

PESTO

 YIELD
about 1 1/2 cups

There's something beautiful about the simplicity of Osteria's pesto: it's shamelessly traditional and universally delicious. They use it in a myriad of different recipes, like pesto-rubbed pork chops, penne with cherry tomatoes, and of course pizzas and flatbreads.

 TIME
Total Time: 10 minutes
Active Time: 10 minutes

INGREDIENTS

3 large bunches of basil (about 6 cups of leaves or 250 grams)
1 tablespoon lemon juice
3/4 cup (100 grams) pine nuts
3 garlic cloves, peeled and roughly chopped
Pinch of black pepper
1/4 teaspoon salt, plus more to taste
1 1/4 cup (300 mL) olive oil

 PREPARATION

1. Blend the basil: Place the basil leaves in the bowl of a food processor. Blend for about 30 seconds, until the basil is very finely chopped.

2. Finish: Add the lemon juice, pine nuts, garlic, black pepper, and salt. With the motor running, slowly pour in one half of the olive oil. Scrape down the sides and then blend again, drizzling in more olive oil until you reach the desired consistency.

3. Serve: Use the pesto with slices of bread, mozzarella, and sliced cherry tomatoes for a beautiful appetizer platter. Or, spread it generously on pizza dough with toppings of your choice.

NOTES

Make your pesto thicker or thinner based on what you'll be serving it with. If it's to be used as a spread on bread or with slices of fresh mozzarella, make it thicker by using just 75% of the olive oil called for in this recipe; if it's going to be used as a pasta sauce, add the full amount of olive oil to thin it.

~~~ OSTERIA ~~~

MOZZARELLA

YIELD
2 large balls (about 14 ounces / 400 grams in total)

TIME
Total Time: 1 hour
Active Time: 40 minutes

SPECIAL TOOLS
Cheesecloth

INGREDIENTS
1 1/4 cup (300 mL) water, divided
1 1/2 teaspoons citric acid
1/4 teaspoon liquid rennet
8 cups (2 litres) whole milk
1 teaspoon salt
Plenty of water, for cooking & cooling
Ice cubes

Mozzarella requires some planning and patience to make at home, but the results are worth it.

PREPARATION

1. Prepare the citric acid and rennet: In a small bowl, measure 1 cup of water. Add the citric acid and stir until it dissolves completely. In another small bowl, measure the remaining 1/4 cup of water. Add the rennet and stir to incorporate.

2. Heat the milk: In a large pot, combine the milk and the citric acid solution. Warm the milk, stirring it gently, over medium heat until it reaches 90F (32C). Then, take the pot off the heat and add the rennet solution. Stir gently for about a minute, then cover the pot and let it sit undisturbed for five minutes.

3. Cut the curds: After five minutes, the milk will have thickened into curds. Use a large knife to make a grid of cuts through the curds, making sure that you go all the way to the bottom of the pot.

4. Separate the curds & whey: Put the pot back on a burner over medium heat. You are aiming for a temperature of about 105F (40C). Stir very gently as you heat the curds, trying not to break them up too much. After a couple of minutes, you will see the curds separating more fully from the yellowish, watery whey.

5. Strain the curds: Line a fine-mesh strainer with cheesecloth. Use a slotted spoon to scoop the curds out of the whey into the strainer. (Save the whey; it's a great way to store finished mozzarella.) Let the curds strain for 30 minutes.

6. Cook the curds: While the curds are straining, heat a large pot of water to a low simmer. Prepare a large bowl of ice water and set it aside. Gather up the ends of the cheesecloth and give the curds a gentle squeeze to remove any extra moisture. Use a piece of kitchen twine to tie up the ends, making a closed bundle. Submerge the bundle in the hot water and leave it there for five minutes. Then, plunge the bundle into the ice water and let the curds cool for about one minute.

7. Knead the curds:
On a clean surface, open your cheesecloth bundle. Sprinkle the teaspoon of salt over the cheese. Remove the curds and knead them gently, as you would bread dough, until they start to feel elastic. (If you are having trouble kneading your curds, it may be because they have cooled too much. Microwave them for 15 seconds and knead again.)

8. Divide: Divide the mozzarella into two pieces. Work each ball of cheese between your hands until it develops a shiny skin on the outside. Shape each piece into a ball.

9. Store or serve: If you aren't going to eat the mozzarella right away, place the cheese in a container and pour extra whey over it to cover completely. Sprinkle a pinch of salt into the whey, cover, and store in the fridge for up to three days. When you're ready to eat the cheese, cut it into rounds and serve on a platter with fresh, sliced tomatoes, a pot of pesto, and grilled bread; or, slice the rounds and spread them on pizza.

Tin Tin

I first met Jamie Pujara at an Indian Kenyan-owned, American franchise pizza shop in Nairobi's Westlands neighborhood. We struck up a conversation about his family and how he is half Indian and half Chinese and is married to a half Dutch half Tanzanian woman, making their young son a quarter Indian, a quarter Chinese, a quarter Dutch, a quarter Tanzanian and one hundred percent Kenyan.

Jamie is the third generation owner of TinTin Restaurant, a Chinese restaurant located in the Kenya International Conference Center (KICC), the tallest building in Nairobi. An enterprising child, he used to get food from the restaurant delivered to him at school, which he would then sell to his classmates. He went to high school and university in the UK and worked as a banker before moving to Japan to teach English and New York to study film. He returned to Kenya to manage the restaurant after his father was diagnosed with cancer.

The restaurant is a family business from top to bottom: of his fifty employees, seven have fathers who also worked at TinTin. They have served every Kenyan president, including the first and second Kenyatta presidents. (President Moi even requested that one of TinTin's chefs go to the State House to train his chefs on how to make their chicken wings.)

In many ways, Jamie is the product of a legacy that can only be described as the quintessential immigrant success story. His grandfather, James Tin, grew up poor in mainland China. When James' father died, his mother took him and his four siblings to live in Hong Kong. World War II was approaching and fearful that the Japanese would invade, his mother put him, her eldest son, on a ship to India. He was sixteen. He arrived in Bombay and didn't like it, so he got back on the boat as a stowaway, not knowing where he would end up next.

James arrived in the port of Mombasa hungry and unimaginably far from home. At the time, Kenya was a British colony, and it was just his luck that the British officer at the port had spent time in Hong Kong and spoke some Cantonese. He took pity on the boy, stamping his papers and helping him to find a job in the shipyard. It was in this same shipyard where, three years later, he met his wife, then sixteen, who was also Chinese.

They eventually had four children together and James spent his career working as an engineer for a shipping company on the coast. In 1977 when he retired, his friend, a successful nightclub impresario, encouraged him to open a restaurant in Nairobi in the newly built KICC building. James loved to entertain and would regularly host three-day long mahjong tournaments with friends at his house. It made sense to open a restaurant. Clearly not one to shy away from an adventure, James jumped on the opportunity and on April 5th, 1978, TinTin opened its doors to the public. James worked the front of the house, his wife was in the kitchen, and his children-- Jamie's mother and her three siblings-- helped wherever they were needed. This was a family business from the start.

Jamie's parents met in Mombasa, where his father worked for a shipping company. His father is Indian, and his grandparents weren't supportive of their relationship. Interracial marriages were rare at the time, and are still unusual in Kenya today. Eventually they eloped in Germany, where his father had found a job, but when Jamie's grandmother died, they returned to Kenya to help with the business. Jamie's father was raised as a pure vegetarian, and brought his own Indian influences to the cuisine at TinTin.

The Tin family represents so beautifully the diversity and the complexity of immigrant life here in Nairobi. Here was a young man forced to leave his home and venture out to create a life for himself. He accidentally ended up in a country he'd probably never heard of before and, through luck and hard work, created a multi-generational institution.

CAI LAN CHAO SHI

FRIED PORK DUMPLINGS

 MAKES
About 4 dozen dumplings

Don't be intimidated by folding dumplings: it's perfectly acceptable to simply fold them in half and press the edges closed with the tines of a fork, as you do for ravoili. These dumplings can be prepared ahead of time and then frozen for up to 3 months. When you're ready to cook them, simply drop them into boiling water straight out of the freezer and boil until they float.

 TIME
Total Time: 45 minutes
Active Time: 45 minutes

 INGREDIENTS
1 1/3 pounds (600 grams) ground pork
Half a head of napa cabbage, grated
1 bunch green onions, minced
1 teaspoon ginger, minced or grated
2 tablespoons soy sauce
1 tablespoon Chinese cooking wine (or dry Sherry)
1 teaspoon sesame oil
1 1/2 teaspoons salt
Round dumpling wrappers (see note)
2 tablespoons neutral oil
1/2 cup (120 mL) water
Soy sauce and vinegar, to serve

 PREPARATION

1. Make the filling: In a large bowl, mix together the pork, cabbage, green onions and ginger. Add the soy sauce, cooking wine, sesame oil, and salt.

2. Fold the dumplings: Place a wrapper on a clean work surface. Using a small spoon or chopsticks, place about a teaspoon of filling in the center of the wrapper. Lightly brush water over the edges of the wrapper and fold it in half. Pinch the edges closed, folding them into a fan shape if you wish.

3. Cook: Heat a nonstick pan over very high heat. Add the 1 tablespoon of oil and arrange the dumplings in the pan so that they fit snugly; you'll have to do multiple batches. Cover and turn the heat to low. Cook for 2 minutes. Then, add the water and immediately cover to trap the steam inside the pan. Cook until most of the liquid is gone, about 5 minutes. Remove the lid and cook 1-2 minutes more, until no more water remains in the bottom of the pan.

4. Serve: Transfer the dumplings to a plate. Serve with small bowls of soy sauce and vinegar, for dipping.

NOTES
You can buy dumpling wrappers at many grocery stores and Chinese markets, but you can also easily make them at home. Simply combine 1 cup (130 grams) all-purpose flour, a pinch of salt, and ½ cup (120 mL) boiling water in a large, heatproof bowl. Stir until it comes together, adding flour as necessary to make a soft, pliable dough. Knead it gently for 2-3 minutes, then cut the dough into small pieces and roll them into thin (about 1/8" thick) circles.

26 | APPETIZERS

CAI LAN CHAO SHI

SEAFOOD WONTONS

SERVES
4-6, as an appetizer or light main

Like dumplings, these wontons can be made ahead of time and frozen. The best freezing method is to place the wontons on a parchment paper-lined sheet in the freezer; once they're completely frozen, transfer them to a tightly sealed plastic baggie. They can be boiled straight out of the freezer in whatever quantity you want.

TIME
Total Time: 45 minutes
Active Time: 45 minutes

PREPARATION

1. **Make the filling:** In a large bowl, mix together the shrimp, pork, green onions, and ginger. Add the soy sauce and salt.

2. **Fold the wontons:** Place a wrapper on a clean work surface. Using a small spoon or chopsticks, place about a teaspoon of filling in the center of the wrapper. Brush some water over the edges of the wrapper and fold it to form a triangle. Add another dab of water to the bottom two corners of the triangle and bring them together, pressing firmly to adhere.

3. **Cook:** Bring a large pot of lightly salted water to a boil and add the wontons. You might have to do this in batches depending on the size of your pot. Cook for 3-5 minutes, or until the wontons float to the top.

4. **Serve:** Transfer the wontons to a bowl. Spoon a couple of tablespoons of the cooking water over the wontons. Sprinkle a little soy sauce over and garnish with green onions.

INGREDIENTS

7 ounces (200 grams) shrimp, peeled and finely chopped

14 ounces (400 grams) ground pork

4 green onions, minced

1 teaspoon grated ginger

2 tablespoons soy sauce, plus more to taste

2 teaspoons salt

1 package square wonton wrappers (storebought or homemade; see page 26)

Green onions, to garnish

~~~ D'AFRIC ~~~

FUUL MEDAMES (FAVA BEAN DIP)

SERVES
about 6, as an appetizer or side

D'Afric's fuul deserves a place in any rotation of dips and spreads. The use of roasted sesame oil gives it a wonderful depth. Make fuul a day ahead if you can: resting it overnight in the fridge allows the flavors to meld beautifully.

TIME
Total Time: 20 minutes
Active Time: 20 minutes

INGREDIENTS
1 pound (450 grams) cooked fava beans (or butter beans, if you can't find favas)
1 teaspoon salt, plus more to taste
1/2 cup (120 mL) roasted sesame oil
1/3 cup (50 grams) crumbled goat cheese

PREPARATION

1. Mash: Divide the cooked fava beans in two. Use a fork to roughly mash one half; place the other half in a food processor and blend until it's very smooth. Mix the two parts back together in a medium bowl. Add the salt, sesame oil, crumbled feta cheese, and chili flakes. Add the tomato and onion, if you're using them. Taste; add additional salt, feta, or chili to your liking.

2. Serve: Serve fuul with bread, chips, or sliced vegetables.

NOTES

1. If you're boiling your own beans, cook them until they're very soft: it will make the mashing & blending easier and result in a creamier fuul.

2. In Sudanese cuisine, both fuul and salata aswat (page 32) are served as main dishes. To enjoy them that way, increase the quantities by half and serve them with bread.

D'AFRIC

SALATA ASWAT (ROASTED EGGPLANT DIP)

 SERVES
4-6, as an appetizer or side

This dish has much in common with Baba Ghanoush (see page 10), but with the essential additions of peanutbutter and minced tomato and onion.

 TIME
Total Time: 40 minutes
Active Time: 20 minutes

 PREPARATION

1. Roast the eggplants. You can do this in one of two ways:
  • In the oven: Turn your broiler to high heat. Place the whole eggplants on a baking sheet just under the broiler. Roast the eggplants, turning them every 2-3 minutes, until the skin is black on all sides, about 15 minutes total.
  • Over a gas stove: Turn the gas on high on two (or three) burners. Place the eggplants directly over the open flame. Turn them every 2-3 minutes, until the skin is thoroughly blackened on all sides, about 15 minutes total.

2. Peel the eggplants: Place the roasted eggplants in a bowl and cover with a lid or cloth. (Trapping the moisture in this way makes it easier to peel the skins away from the eggplants.) Once the eggplants are cool, cut off their stems and peel off the blackened skins. Discard the skins.

3. Blend: Use a fork to thoroughly mash the eggplant. Add the lemon juice, tahini paste, and peanut butter and stir until the mixture is smooth. Add the parsley, tomato, onion, hot pepper, about a teaspoon of salt, and a pinch of pepper. Taste; add more salt or lemon to your liking.

4. Serve: Enjoy salata aswat with bread, chips, or vegetable sticks.

 INGREDIENTS
2 large eggplants (or 3 smaller ones)
Juice of one lemon (about 1 tablespoon)
1 cup (200 grams) tahini paste
2 tablespoons peanut butter
1/2 cup (25 grams) fresh parsley, minced
1 tomato, finely chopped
1 yellow onion, minced
1 small hot pepper, minced
Salt and pepper, to taste

Open House

Anil and Matthew have owned and operated Open House, one of Nairobi's most celebrated restaurants, for over twenty-five years, but both agree that their greatest joy is their friendship. While solo restaurateurs are common in Nairobi, just as frequently restaurants are started by best friends. There's a special relationship between business partners and best friends, but what makes these stories even more special is that they left their home countries together to forge a new life somewhere else, together.

Anil and Matthew grew up in different parts of India, Anil in the North and Matthew in the South, but they met while working in high-end hotels in Bombay. One started out cleaning bathrooms and the other butchering animals, and they both moved their way up to becoming chefs. They ended up in Kenya somewhat by accident, when they decided to take a holiday somewhere, and Kenya was one of the few countries in the world where they could get a visa on arrival. So in 1987, they landed in Nairobi preparing to stay for a few weeks, but at the encouragement of school friends here, they decided to stay, and quickly found jobs cooking in a restaurant. After eight years, they finally had the savings and citizenship to open a restaurant of their own, which they named Open House.

Open House is tucked away in an office block in Westlands, with a small sign hanging over the door letting hungry diners know that they're at the right place. The kitchen is filled with a loud din of roaring fires, sizzling meats and endless chopping. There's hardly space to move, but everyone has a role and within a few minutes of an order being called in, the food is ready.

When they first opened, they had to convince people in the neighborhood to try their food, since most families had cooks at home. Being chefs, they knew how to make delicious food, but the challenge was in figuring out how to adapt to local tastes and ingredients. They found the onions to be sweeter than what they were used to in India, and the ginger more flavorful. They both talked about how they love to experiment and create new dishes, and twenty-four years later, they have customers who treat Open House like their own homes. They both fondly talked about customers whose orders their servers have memorized, and children that they've seen grow into adults (whose parents order food frozen to ship to their nostalgic children abroad). They have one customer who has eaten the same dish four times a week for eighteen years. They have another who has been coming in twice a week for eight years. Matthew showed me a customer who is saved in his phone as simply "Chili Paneer," the dish that he always orders.

Open House is Matthew and Anil's home – they're everyone's reassuring uncles, always eager to feed you something delicious and make sure you're happy. Their passion for their work is evident, in talking about the food they make, the customers they serve and the team they employ. The distance they've traveled from being lowly employees in India to owning a successful restaurant in Nairobi is enormous.

Matthew said that when he told his family he was opening a restaurant, his father imagined him running a little chai kiosk. Little did his father know this chai kiosk would eventually raise a daughter who became a doctor, a son who became an engineer, and an entire community that just can't get enough chili paneer.

——— FURUSATO ———

TEMPURA PRAWNS

SERVES
6, as an appetizer

These crunchy, flavorful prawns are a a perfect party food or start to a meal. Serve with the dipping sauce listed.

TIME
Total Time: 20 minutes
Active Time: 20 minutes

INGREDIENTS FOR THE PRAWNS

1 cup (240 mL) cold water
1 cup (130 grams) white flour
1 egg yolk
1/2 teaspoon baking soda
1 teaspoon salt
2 1/4 pounds (1 kg) jumbo prawns, peeled & deveined
2 tablespoons cornstarch
1/2 cup (120 mL) neutral oil

FOR THE DIPPING SAUCE

1 tablespoon finely grated ginger
3 green onions, chopped
2 tablespoons grated daikon radish
2 tablespoons soy sauce
1/2 cup (120 mL) dashi broth (see note)
Pinch of sugar

PREPARATION

1. Make the batter:
In a medium bowl, combine the water, flour, egg yolk, baking soda, and salt.

2. Prep the prawns: Rinse the prawns, then squeeze excess moisture from them and pat them dry with a paper towel. Toss them in the cornstarch.

3. Fry the prawns: In a large pan, heat the oil. Test the oil by dropping a teaspoon of tempura batter in it; if it immediately sizzles, the oil is ready. Dunk each prawn into the tempura batter, then carefully place it in the oil. (You may have to do this in multiple batches, as you don't want to crowd the prawns as they fry.) Let them cook for 2-3 minutes, until the bottom side is nicely browned. Flip and cook for another 2-3 minutes, until the tempura batter has browned all over. Place the cooked prawns on a paper towel-lined plate.

5. Make the dipping sauce: Combine all the sauce ingredients in a medium bowl. Taste and adjust the seasoning to your liking.

6. Serve: Enjoy the prawns & dipping sauce on their own as an appetizer, or toss them into your favorite stir fry.

NOTES

To make dashi broth, first soak 1 ounce (28 grams) kombu (dried kelp) in 4 cups (1 litre) water in a large pot. Let it soak for at least 30 minutes or up to 3 hours. Put the pot over medium high heat; just before the water boils, remove the kombu. Add 2 cups (35 grams) dried bonito flakes, bring to a boil, and then simmer for 30 minutes. Strain the broth through a fine mesh strainer. Discard the bonito flake and use the broth as you would other vegetable or seafood stocks.

~~~ OPEN HOUSE ~~~

CHILLY GARLIC MUSHROOM

SERVES
2-3, as a starter

These mushrooms hit all the marks: they're a little crunchy, salty, and spicy, with a splash of lemon to balance the flavors. They're a perfect bite-sized appetizer.

TIME
Total Time: 45 minutes
Active Time: 45 minutes

INGREDIENTS
7 ounces (200 grams) button mushrooms, thoroughly cleaned
2/3 cup (85 grams) flour
1/2 cup (120 mL) water
1 teaspoon salt
1/4 cup (60 mL) neutral oil
2 tablespoons butter
1 tablespoon minced garlic
1 teaspoon chili powder, plus more to taste
Pinch of black pepper
1 lemon, cut into wedges

PREPARATION

1. Prepare the batter: Mix the water, flour, and salt to make a thick batter.

2. Cook: Heat the oil in a large, heavy-bottomed skillet over high heat. Dip the mushrooms in the batter, then fry for four minutes. Carefully turn the mushrooms and cook for an additional 3 minutes. Scoop the mushrooms onto a paper towel-lined plate and set aside.

3. Finish: In a large skillet, melt the butter. Add the minced garlic, chili powder, and black pepper and cook for 1 minute, until the garlic starts to brown. Toss the mushrooms in tthishe butter and spice mixture for 1-2 minutes. Taste; add a sprinkle of extra chili powder and salt, if desired.

4. Serve: Squeeze a little lemon juice over the mushrooms, then serve the mushrooms with the remaining lemon.

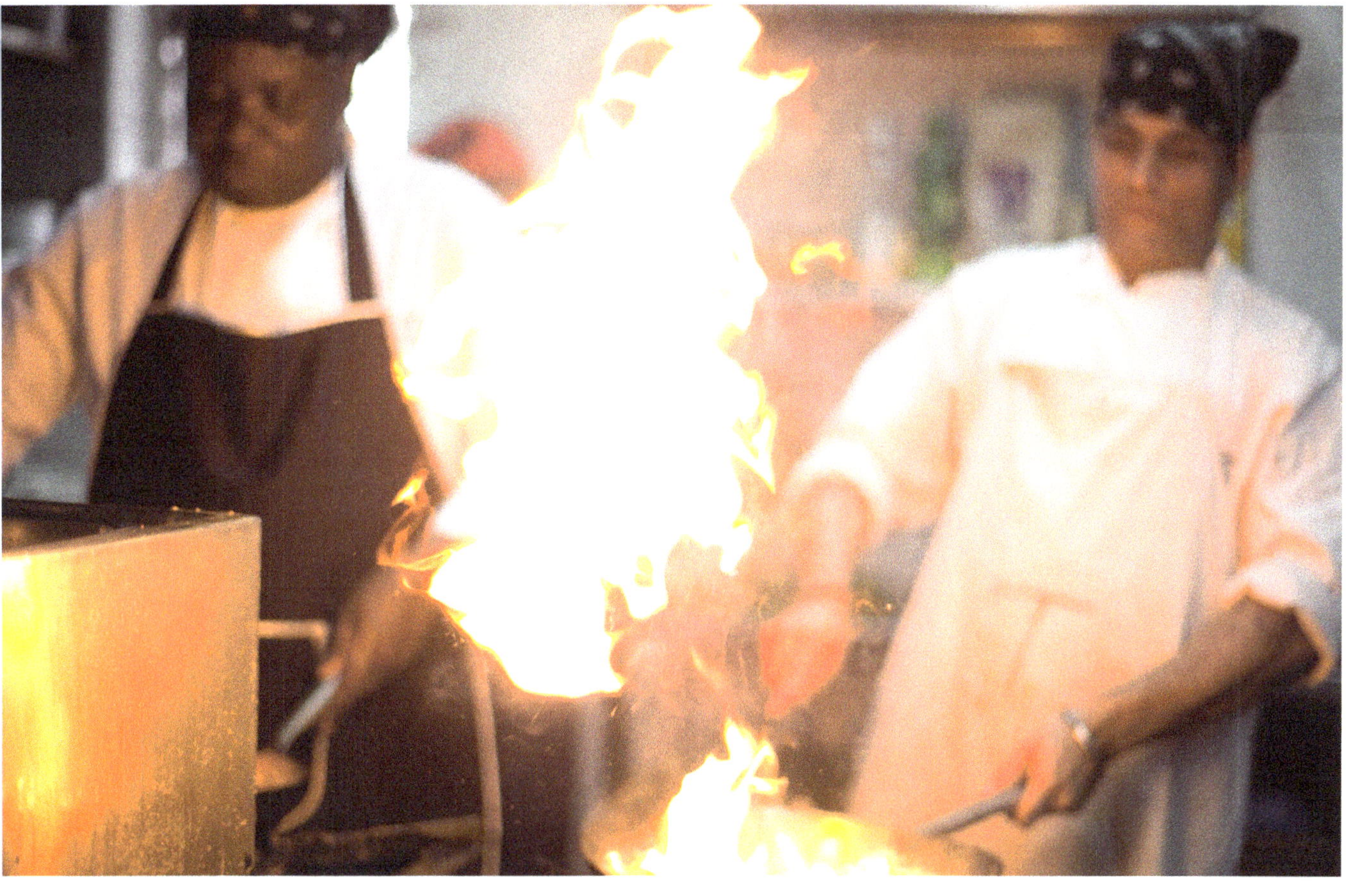

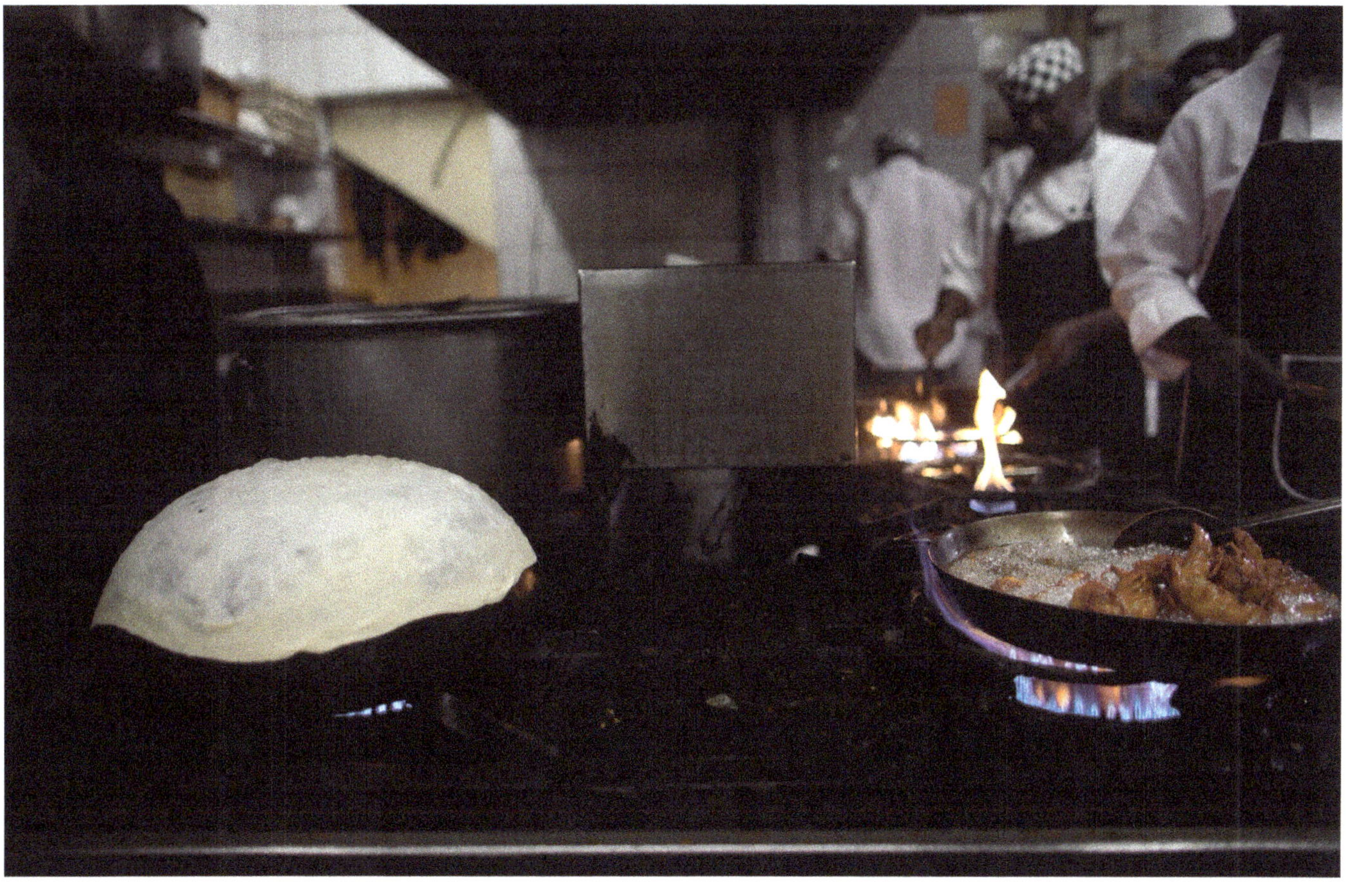

~~ TIN TIN ~~

CHICKEN WINGS

SERVES
3-6, depending on how hungry your group is

Tin Tin roasts their chicken wings and then quickly deep fries them to make them extra crispy before serving. For the home cook, we recommend just tossing the wings in a wok with melted butter after they come out of the oven: you'll get a little extra crisp without all the spattering oil.

TIME
Total Time: 1 hour
Active Time: 20 minutes

INGREDIENTS
2 tablespoons corn flour
2 teaspoons sugar
2 chicken stock cubes, crushed to a powder
2 eggs
2 teaspoons soy sauce
1/4 cup (60 mL) corn oil
1 teaspoon salt
12 chicken wings
1 tablespoon butter
6 whole green onions, chopped

PREPARATION

1. Make the marinade:
Combine the corn flour, sugar, crushed stock cubes, eggs, soy sauce, oil, and salt in a large bowl. Add the chicken wings and coat them well in the sauce. Allow the chicken to marinate for at least 30 minutes, or up to overnight.

2. Cook: Preheat the oven to 400F (200C). Place the marinated chicken wings on a large, tin foil-lined baking sheet. Roast for 12 minutes, turning the chicken halfway through. After 12 minutes, remove one piece and make a small cut to ensure that there is no pink in the middle. (Or, use a thermometer to check that the meat has reached an internal temperature of 160F/70C.) If the meat is not quite cooked through, continue roasting 3-4 minutes more. Once done, remove the chicken wings from the oven and let them cool slightly.

3. Finish: Melt the butter in a large skillet or wok. Add the green onions and cook until they begin to brown. Add the chicken to the pan and toss to coat the wings with the green onions.

4. Serve: Serve with a starch of your choice.

NOTES

If you have an outdoor grill, use it! Grill the chicken over medium - high heat, turning them every 3 - 4 minutes until they are cooked on all sides. Just be sure to check that the chicken is thoroughly cooked through before serving.

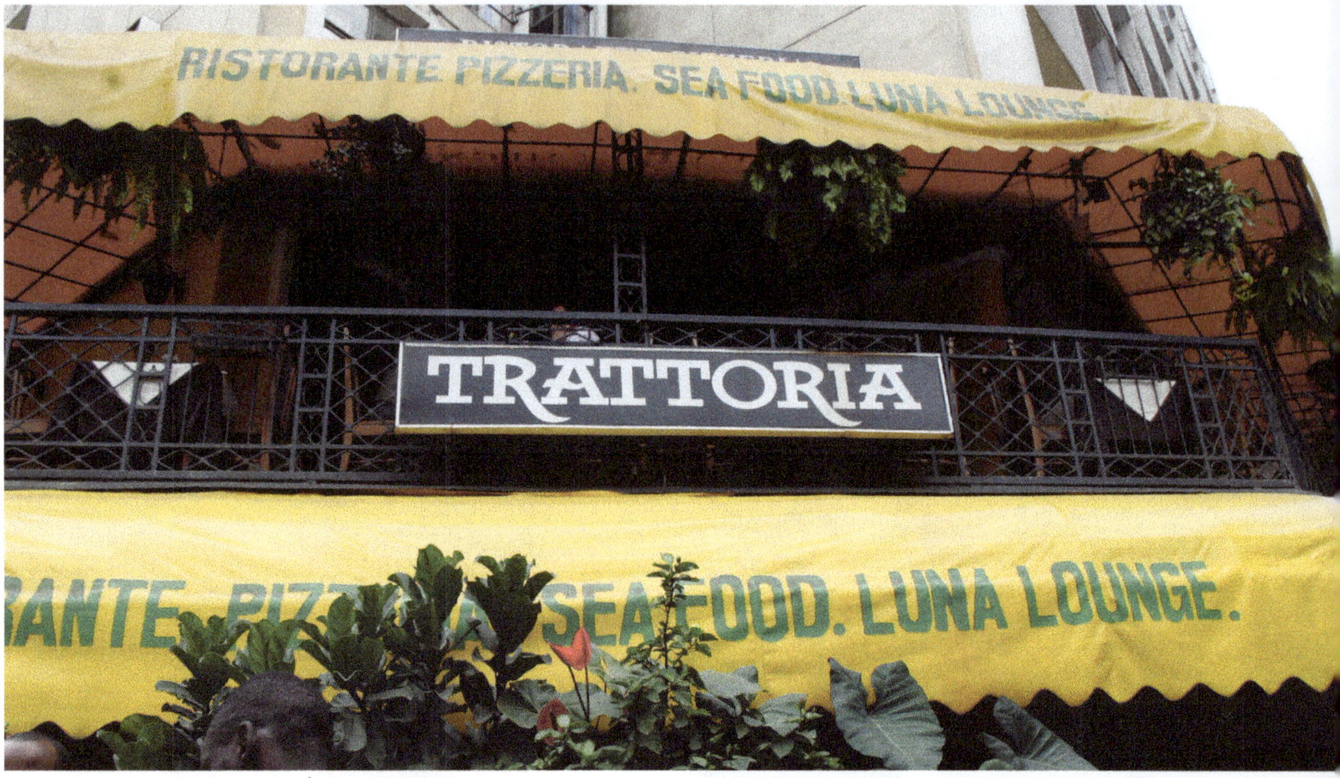
RISTORANTE PIZZERIA. SEA FOOD.
TRATTORIA
SEA FOOD. LUNA LOUNGE.

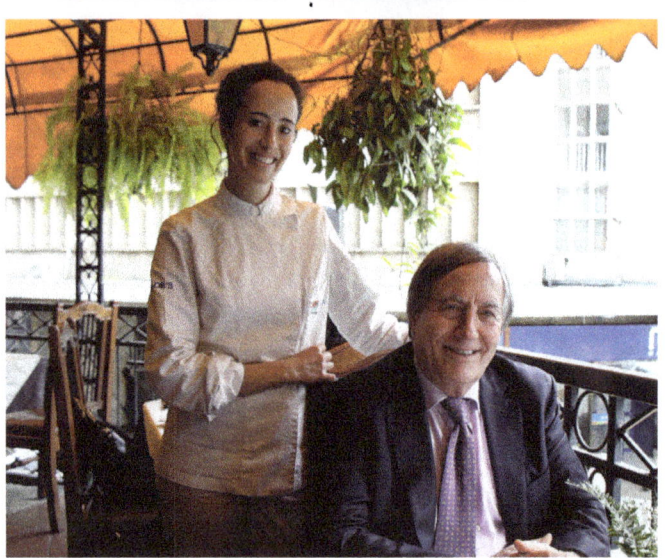

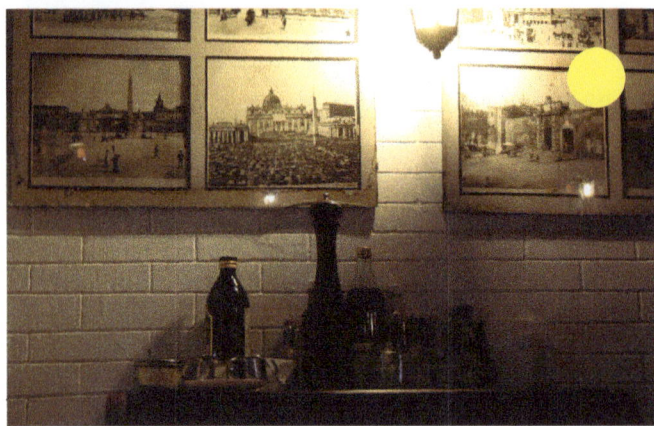

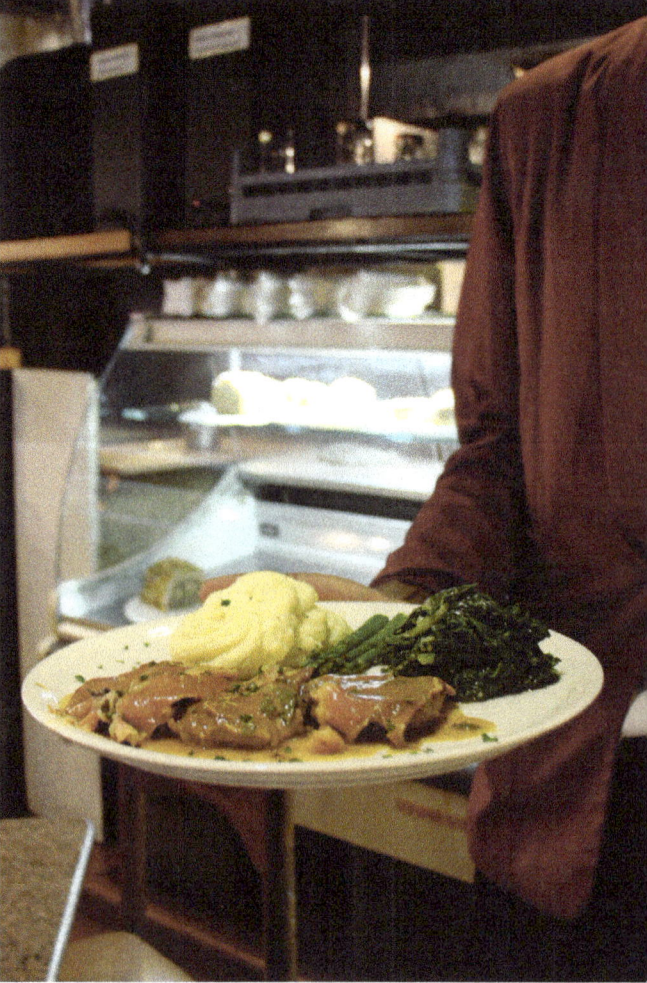

Trattoria

Nightmares brought Gaetano Ruffo back to Nairobi. He'd first traveled to Kenya for three months as a stand-up bass player in the house jazz band at the Intercontinental Hotel, but when he returned to his native Italy, he had terrible dreams and couldn't sleep. He realized that the problem was that he missed Kenya, so he rejoined the band with a plan to stay for a year. Little did he know that one year would turn into forty.

Gaetano grew up in a village in Calabria, so poor that as a child he didn't own a pair of shoes. His family moved to Rome and he trained as an hotelier, but found work as a musician. It's fitting, then, that music brought him to Kenya and food kept him here.

In 1981, he opened a coffee shop in downtown Nairobi and a year later brought his mother from Italy to cook. Just like that, Nairobi's first Italian restaurant, Trattoria, was born. His mother trained their entire staff, teaching them how to make fresh pastas, pizzas, and even mozzarella cheese. She never learned English or Swahili, but her kitchen staff all learned Italian. When she died, she was buried in Rome in a dress made of kitenge, a traditional Kenyan textile.

Trattoria is a restaurant that feels frozen in time. Curing meats hang from the rafters, cheeses sit in a deli display for sale by the kilogram, and fake and real ivy climb along the walls. It's located just across the street from Nairobi City Hall, so at any given time, tables are filled with men in dark suits, discussing important matters over cappuccinos, university students splitting pizza slices, and couples sharing a romantic meal out. When Gaetano talks about the 1982 attempted coup of the Moi government, it's hard to imagine the city under lockdown, but this little oasis of carbs and cured meats kept its doors open, feeding anyone who walked in. He still remembers having his car keys taken from him by protesters and being forced to walk from his home in the suburb of Westlands to his restaurant downtown at gunpoint.

Just being a restaurateur wasn't enough for Gaetano, so he also opened a series of nightclubs. At that time, women weren't allowed into clubs without a man, and he proudly claims that his was the first club in Nairobi to have a ladies night and a dress code (no sneakers).

Trattoria is now a third generation restaurant with his daughter Luna, a formally trained chef who studied hotel management in Switzerland, managing the restaurant. From a woman who had never left Italy and spoke only Italian, to a son whose nightmares drove them to Kenya, to a daughter who grew up around the world, the Ruffo family, like James Tin, are part of a larger immigrant narrative that illustrate Nairobi's multi-faceted history.

~~~ CHEKA ~~~

BRAISED PORK BELLY

SERVES
4, as an appetizer

Pork belly is a fatty cut of meat. For this reason, these servings are very small. The beauty of pork belly is that a few bites leave you pleasantly satisfied. Cheka's preparation is so good, though, that you may be tempted to make a whole meal out of pork belly.

TIME
Total Time: 1 hour 20 minutes
Active Time: 20 minutes

PREPARATION

1. Make the sauce: Whisk together the water, soy sauce, mirin, sake, garlic, ginger, and sugar in a small bowl.

2. Sear the pork: Heat the neutral oil over high heat in a small saucepan. Add the block of pork belly, fattiest side down. Sear for three minutes, then flip and cook for one minute on the other side. Remove the pan from the heat and let it cool for several minutes; then, pour the sauce over, being careful as it may splatter.

3. Simmer: Cover the pot with a heavy lid and return it to very low heat. Simmer for about one hour, checking every 10 minutes to ensure that there is still liquid in the pan. The liquid need not cover the pork entirely, but there should be at least a half inch of liquid in the pan to create steam. If the liquid does evaporate, add water 1/2 cup (120 mL) at a time.

INGREDIENTS
8 ounces (225 grams) pork belly
1 2/3 cup (400 mL) water
3 tablespoons soy sauce
1 tablespoon mirin
1 tablespoon sake
1 teaspoon minced garlic
1 teaspoon minced ginger
1 teaspoon sugar
2 teaspoons neutral oil
2 medium leeks, cleaned and finely sliced
2 tablespoons karashi (or smooth dijon mustard)
Sprinkle of red chili flakes, to garnish

4. Make the salad: While the pork is cooking, toss the sliced leek with the karashi.

5. Finish: After about an hour, remove the pork belly from the pot and let it cool on a cutting board. Raise the heat to medium and boil the remaining liquid until it thickens, 5-7 minutes.

6. Serve: Make a small mound of dressed leeks in the middle of four small plates. Cut the pork belly into 4-8 thin slices and place atop the leek salad. Garnish the plates with a drizzle of the reduced sauce and a sprinkle of red chili.

~ CHEKA ~

FRIED OCTOPUS

 SERVES
4, as a starter

Serving mayonnaise alongside this octopus may seem odd at first, but trust Cheka: the tartness of the mayonnaise is the perfect complement to the rich meat of the octopus.

 TIME
Total Time: 45 minutes
Active Time: About 12 hours

 INGREDIENTS
14 ounces (400 grams) octopus
2 tablespoons coarse salt
2 tablespoons soy sauce
2 tablespoons mirin
2 tablespoons sake
1 teaspoon minced garlic
1 teaspoon minced ginger
1/3 cup (45 grams) all-purpose flour
2 tablespoons cornstarch
2 tablespoons neutral oil
1/4 head white cabbage, finely shredded
1 medium carrot, grated
1/4 cup (55 grams) mayonnaise

 PREPARATION

1. The night before, salt the octopus: Place the octopus in a medium bowl. Sprinkle the salt over, rubbing it gently into the octopus. Let the octopus rest for at least 20 minutes.

2. Make the marinade: While the octopus is brining, mix the soy sauce, mirin, sake, garlic, and ginger together in a medium bowl.

3. Marinate the octopus: Thoroughly rinse the salt off the octopus and gently pat it dry. Cut it into pieces about 1" long and place the pieces in the marinade. Cover and leave in the fridge overnight, or for about 12 hours.

4. Strain: About 20 minutes before serving, remove the octopus from the fridge and strain the octopus out of the marinade. Let it sit in the strainer for a couple of minutes to remove excess liquid.

5. Make the coating: While the octopus is straining, combine the flour and cornstarch in a wide bowl.

6. Fry: Heat the oil over high heat in a wide, heavy bottomed pan. Gently toss each piece of octopus in the coating to cover it on all sides. Carefully place the pieces of octopus in the skillet; depending on the size of your pan, you may have to do this in two batches to avoid crowding the octopus. Cook for 2 minutes, then flip the pieces and cook for an additional minute, until you no longer see any dry coating on the exterior. Place the fried octopus on a paper towel-lined plate to absorb excess grease.

7. Serve: Put the shredded cabbage and carrot in a medium serving dish. Place the octopus atop the vegetables. Serve with the mayonnaise alongside, for dipping.

Soups & Salads

50	TOM YAM KUNG (SWEET & SOUR PRAWN SOUP)	Som Tam Thai
54	OKRA STEW	Bodyzone
56	WINTERMELON SOUP	Tin Tin
58	BEEF NOODLE SOUP	Cai Lan Chao Shi
62	DAILLO	Al Yusra
63	APPLE COLESLAW	Purdy Arms
64	PLUM PECORINO SALAD	Marula Mercantile
66	SOM TAM (GREEN PAPAYA SALAD)	Som Tam Thai
70	CUCUMBER COLD DISH	Han Di Yuan
72	NIGERIAN PEPPER SOUP	Mama Ashanti
74	LA TAGLIATA	La Salumeria
78	SPICY CALAMARI SALAD	Moniko's

~~~ SOM TAM THAI ~~~

TOM YAM KUNG
(SOUR AND SPICY PRAWN SOUP)

 SERVES
4, as an appetizer or very light main

This soup has intense sour and spicy flavors. If you wish, you can add a tablespoon of sugar to balance the acidity and spice.

 TIME
Total Time: 10 minutes
Active Time: 10 minutes

 INGREDIENTS
3 cups (720 mL) shrimp or chicken stock
6 large prawns, shelled and deveined
7 ounces (200 grams) white mushrooms, sliced
1 stem lemongrass, cut into 1-inch pieces
1 tablespoon minced galangal (or ginger)
¼ cup (60 mL) lime juice
3 tablespoons fish sauce

 PREPARATION

1. Make the soup: In a large pot, bring the stock to a boil. Add all the other ingredients and bring back to a boil. Boil just until the shrimp are cooked, about 5 minutes. Taste; add additional salt, lime juice, fish sauce, and chilis to your liking.

2. Serve: Serve with a sprinkle of chopped cilantro.

NOTES

This soup is delicious with chicken or fish as well. Simply replace the prawns with 8 ounces (225 grams) of cubed chicken breast or fresh fish (we like snapper or rock cod).

50 | SOUPS & SALADS

Cedars

Magne Albrightsen grew up on an island in Norway so far north that it's in the Arctic Circle. Growing up the son of a fisherman, he knew little more than his island and the ocean around it. As soon as he was old enough, he enlisted in the army so that he could see the world.

From the Norwegian army, he joined the UN Peacekeeping Operations, traveling to nearly every major conflict zone in Africa and the Middle East in the 1980s and 90s. He was in Burundi when war broke out, Angola during the civil war, Rwanda during the genocide, Sudan during independence, and Iraq, Lebanon, Iran--really, everywhere. He met his wife in Lebanon, and when he left the Peacekeeping Operations to join another branch of the UN, they moved to Nairobi together. When asked why they decided on Nairobi, Magne responded, with a look as if offended by the obviousness of the answer, "It's a paradise!"

After over twenty years working for the UN as a peacekeeper and then a communications technician, he decided that he was ready to do something on his own. Along with partners, he started a satellite communications company in Sudan and later decided that he wanted to open a restaurant. He'd found the perfect space, an old bungalow on an acre of mature garden just across the street from Osteria and the original Misono. His wife's cousin Elie would come from Lebanon to be the chef. In 1994, Cedars, Nairobi's first Lebanese restaurant, was born.

Today Nairobi's supermarkets, green grocers and specialty stores sell just about everything – enough to satisfy even the most discerning chef from nearly every cuisine. There's a Korean supermarket that sells all manners of noodles and sauces. An Italian shop that sells pastas, salamis, even organic Italian wines. Diamond Plaza and South Asian shops all over the city sell spices, locally grown curry leaves, and galangal. But when Magne was setting up Cedars, he couldn't even find parsley. There's no Lebanese food without tabbouleh, so he managed to smuggle seeds in from Lebanon and distribute them to farmers outside of the city, promising to buy whatever they grew. He had to be similarly inventive with other ingredients like olive oil and tahini, and managed to source well enough to satisfy his Lebanese chef.

In some ways, Cedars feels like a clubhouse with its low lighting and crimson tablecloths. The wait staff wear starched dress shirts with ties, and move gracefully around the dining room with trays piled high with mezze. Magne holds court daily at the restaurant, checking in on the kitchens, chatting with Kioko, the barman who started at Cedars on day one as a teenage cleaner, and lunching on salmon with his wife and children, who help out with the business. Salmon, while not Lebanese, makes an appearance on the menu because Magne is insistent about his Norwegian love for fish. He even started a Norwegian seafood import business on the side, overnighting fresh salmon to feed Nairobi's growing appetite for sushi and expensive seafood.

A proud Norwegian, Magne cures salmon for his family, makes his own lamb rullepølse (rolled and cured lamb), and can talk for hours about boats and sailing. Nairobi is home, his children and his grandchildren are here, and his English is speckled with Swahili. But in many ways Magne is still the boy from the island, eager for his father to come home from the sea with exotic gifts and fresh fish. He has seen the world, and now he's home.

~~~ BODY ZONE ~~~

OKRA STEW

SERVES
2-3 as a main,
or 4-6 as a first course

A fascinating distinction between cuisines is the way to thicken soups and sauces. In French cuisine, the béchamel reigns supreme; Chinese cooking prefers cornstarch slurries; Nigerian food uses blended beans. Congolese cuisine, like many other central and Western African countries, frequently uses okra as a thickener.

TIME
Total Time: 20 minutes
Active Time: 20 minutes

INGREDIENTS
4 tomatoes, roughly chopped
2 sweet red peppers, seeded and chopped
½ cup (120 mL) water
6 tablespoons neutral oil
12 ounces (340 grams) okra, cut into very small pieces
3 yellow onions, minced
1 ½ teaspoons salt, plus more to taste
½ teaspoon black pepper
1 teaspoon chili powder (optional)
½ teaspoon baking soda

PREPARATION

1. Blend the tomato and pepper: Place the tomatoes, red peppers, and water in a blender. Blend until it is fairly smooth, then set the mixture aside.

2. Make the stew: Heat the oil in a large pan over medium-high heat. Add the okra and fry until the pieces just begin to brown, about 5 minutes, then add the onions and stir until the onions are soft, about 3 minutes more. Add the blended tomato and pepper, taking care as the sauce may splatter. Stir in the salt, pepper, and chili powder. Simmer for about 20 minutes, stirring occasionally, until the soup has thickened slightly. Turn off the heat and add the baking soda. Taste; add salt and pepper to your liking.

3. Serve: Serve okra stew with a side of rice tand fried plantains (page 196).

NOTES

The baking soda in this recipe creates air bubbles that lighten the stew. You can omit it if you prefer, but Bodyzone's chef stresses that the baking soda is key to good okra stew.

~ TIN TIN ~

WINTERMELON SOUP

SERVES
3 - 4, as a light starter

If you've never had a melon soup before, now is the time to try. This soup comes together in under 20 minutes and, with its unique combination of flavors, is guaranteed to impress. Don't skimp on the green onions at the end; they are essential for crunch and color.

TIME
Total Time: 1 hour
Active Time: 20 minutes

INGREDIENTS
1 low-sodium chicken stock cube
1 teaspoon salt
2 teaspoons granulated sugar
3 cups (720 mL) water
1/4 winter melon (about 5 ounces / 150 grams), peeled and cut into small cubes
1 chicken breast, cut into small pieces
6 whole green onions, chopped

PREPARATION

1. Make the stock: In a small bowl, crush the stock cube with a fork. Add the salt and sugar and stir to mix well. Tip this mixture into a medium pot and add the water. Bring the water to a boil.

2. Cook the melon & chicken: When the water comes to a boil, add the winter melon. Boil for 10 minutes, until the melon is very tender and just starting to fall apart. Add the chicken and boil another 8 - 9 minutes, until the chicken pieces are cooked through.

3. Finish: Add the chopped green onions and boil for one more minute. Ladle into small bowls and serve.

~~ CAI LAN CHAO SHI ~~

BEEF NOODLE SOUP

SERVES

4-6

TIME

Total Time: 3 - 4 hours
Active Time: 35 minutes

INGREDIENTS

2 pounds (900 grams) beef bones, with marrow

8 cups (2 litres) water, plus more

1 pound (450 grams) brisket or other flavorful cut of beef

1 inch knob of ginger, peeled and sliced

4 garlic cloves, peeled and crushed

1 teaspoon Sichuan peppercorns

2 cinnamon sticks

5 whole star anise

1 teaspoon sugar

1 teaspoon dark soy sauce

1 tablespoon light soy sauce

2 tablespoons Chinese cooking wine (or dry Sherry)

10-12 ounces (285-340 grams) dry noodles

4-5 bulbs of baby bok choi, roughly chopped

Chopped green onions and cilantro, to garnish

PREPARATION

1. Make beef stock: Place the beef bones in a large stockpot, cover with water, and bring to a boil. Skim off the scum from the top and add more water, about 8 cups in total. Bring to a boil a second time and then simmer for at least 1 hour, or for up to 5 hours, adding water as needed to keep the bones covered. Strain out the bones and reserve the liquid.

2. Cook the brisket: In another, smaller pot, cover the brisket with water and bring it to a boil. Immediately pour out that water and scum and refill the pot to just cover the meat. Add the ginger, garlic, Sichuan peppercorns, cinnamon, star anise, sugar, soy sauces, and cooking wine. Simmer over very low heat for 2-3 hours, adding water as needed to keep the brisket covered, then remove the brisket and set it on a cutting board to cool. Bring the liquid back to a boil and boil until it has decreased in volume by about half. Turn off the heat and reserve the liquid. Slice the brisket into very thin slices.

3. Blanch the bok choi: Bring a medium pot of lightly salted water to a boil. Add the bok choi and boil for about 1 minute. Rinse the bok choi in cold water and set it aside.

4. Prepare the noodles: Boil the noodles in a separate pot according to the package instructions. Once they're al dente, divide them among your serving bowls.

5. Serve: Top the noodles with a cup of beef stock and a few spoonfuls of the reserved brisket cooking liquid. Place several pieces of sliced brisket on top of the noodles, then garnish with blanched bok choi, cilantro and green onions.

NOTES

You can choose to use one of many wheat-based noodles in this recipe. Standard spaghetti will work fine, as will udon, ramen, or soba noodles.

58 | SOUPS & SALADS

Chowpaty

Ashok Panderi moved to Nairobi twenty four years ago when he was hired to be a manager in a restaurant in Diamond Plaza, a shopping center in the heart of Nairobi's South Asian community. He grew up in the city of Udipi in South India and from a young age started working in restaurants. Coincidentally, he and Matthew, the owner of Open House, grew up just 30 meters apart in the same town, though their journeys to Kenya were completely separate.

In 1995, Ashok decided to open his own restaurant in Diamond Plaza, and Chowpaty was born. He started with four tables in a small stall and served only vegetarian food. As the business grew, he brought a chef from India and hired staff. Today, Chowpaty has four locations, employing over 250 people. Fourteen years ago, he met and married his wife, Sapna, and they operate the business together, rotating between all the restaurant locations.

The sheer scale of production at Chowpaty is mind-blowing. Everything is made from raw materials that are sourced from around Nairobi, with the exception of spices, which are imported from India. They mill their own flours for everything from the idli and dosas, to parathas and naans. They make nine to ten kilos of paneer a day, going through over two hundred liters of milk each time. All the food in the restaurant is made to order, meaning that it's possible to have a meal where everything was harvested and prepared the same day.

For much of Nairobi's South Asian vegetarian community, eating at Chowpaty is part of a family routine. Often when sitting in the restaurants, you'll be surrounded by people young and old, families, couples, groups of teenagers, all happily passing around dishes that they grew up with. Sapna mentioned that it's not rare to get a request for frozen paneer tikka from parents who want to send a taste of home to their children living or studying abroad.

Diamond Plaza feels like a little India. Walking in through the food court entrance, you're immediately hit with the smell of spices and frying samosas. You'll pass hawkers selling coconuts, ready to open one up for you to drink right then and there. You'll see a man shaving betel nut for fresh paan, and when you reach the mall itself and you'll be confronted with floors and floors of shops selling everything from South Asian clothing and shoes to electronics. In many ways it's fitting that Chowpaty started here as a dream, grew to a small stand, and now is a beloved institution in the heart of Nairobi.

~~~ AL YUSRA ~~~

DIALLO (BRAISED GOAT)

SERVES
4-6

This hearty stew requires a lot of time but very little effort. It is traditionally served as the anchor of a meal with a generous side of rice.

TIME
Total Time: 8+ hours
Active Time: 15 minutes

INGREDIENTS

2 pounds (900 grams) tender goat meat (or lamb), cut into bite-sized cubes
2 tablespoons olive oil
1 tablespoon curry powder
1 tablespoon minced garlic
1 teaspoons minced ginger
6-8 tomatoes, roughly chopped
2 yellow onions, chopped
2 tablespoons soy sauce
Large handful of cilantro, roughly chopped
Salt, to taste
2 cups cooked white rice (optional)

PREPARATION

1. **Brown the meat:** Heat the oil in a medium pan over high heat. Sear the meat on all sides, then remove it from the heat.

2. **Braise:** Place the meat, curry powder, garlic, ginger, tomatoes, and onions in the bowl of a slow cooker or Dutch oven. Simmer over very low heat for at least 8 hours, until the meat is very tender.

3. **Serve:** Stir the soy sauce into the stew. Taste; add salt to your liking. Sprinkle with chopped cilantro and serve with rice (or Somali rice, page 82).

NOTES

If you don't have a slow cooker or Dutch oven, you can use a heavy pot with a good lid. Just be sure to keep the heat very low and to add water occasionally if the level is getting low.

APPLE COLESLAW SALAD

SERVES
6

This fresh, healthy salad comes together in just minutes. It's perfect for picnics, packed lunches, and barbecues.

TIME
Total Time: 10 minutes
Active Time: 10 minutes

INGREDIENTS

1/4 head of white cabbage, grated
1/4 head of red cabbage, grated
2 large carrots, grated
1 yellow onion, minced
1 green apple, thinly sliced
1 tablespoon lemon juice
1/4 cup (55 grams) mayonnaise
Salt and pepper, to taste

PREPARATION

1. Make the coleslaw: In a large bowl, combine the red and white cabbage, carrots, onion, and apple. Squeeze the lemon juice over the apple to keep it from browning. Add the mayonnaise and stir everything together. Taste; add salt and pepper as desired.

2. Serve: Serve coleslaw as an accompaniment to burgers (page 164), chicken wings (page 40), or steak skewers (page 176).

MARULA MERCANTILE

PLUM & PECORINO SALAD WITH WALNUT VINAIGRETTE

SERVES
4-6

You may think that the amount of dressing for this salad seems high. Trust Marula Mercantile on this one: this dressing truly makes the salad. If you're convinced it's too much, you can save the dressing for another use, but don't be shy about using it all.

TIME
Total Time: 20 minutes
Active Time: 20 minutes

INGREDIENTS FOR THE DRESSING
1 cup (75 grams) walnuts
2 shallots, minced
1/2 cup (50 grams) finely grated pecorino
1 tablespoon honey
1/3 cup + 2 tablespoons (110 mL) apple cider vinegar
1/2 teaspoon salt

FOR THE SALAD
2 heads of little gem or baby romaine lettuce, washed and with the stems removed
Small handful of chives and parsley, minced
2 large plums, or several smaller ones, pitted and chopped
Large handful (about 3 ounces / 85 grams) shaved pecorino
1/2 cup + 2 tablespoons (150 mL) olive oil

PREPARATION

1. Toast the walnuts: Toast the walnuts in a pan over medium-low heat, stirring occasionally, until they are quite aromatic and begin to turn dark golden, about 5 minutes. Set them aside to cool for a couple of minutes, then roughly chop them.

2. Make the dressing: Combine the walnuts, minced shallots, grated pecorino, honey, apple cider vinegar, and salt in a medium bowl. Stir to combine, then slowly whisk in the olive oil.

3. Serve: Tear up the salad greens a bit; place them in a large bowl along with the chives and parsley. Toss the greens with the dressing to coat thoroughly, then top with the plums and shaved pecorino.

SOM TAM (GREEN PAPAYA SALAD)

SERVES
4-6

This bright, fresh salad is a mainstay of Thai cuisine. It is a perfect example of the philosophy of balance that drives Thai cooking, combining sweet, sour, and salty in a single dish.

TIME
Total Time: 15 minutes
Active Time: 10 minutes

INGREDIENTS

1 green papaya, peeled and coarsely shredded

1/2 carrot, peeled and shredded

3.5 ounces (100 grams) French beans, cut into 1-inch pieces

3.5 ounces (100 grams) cherry tomatoes, halved

2 tablespoons peanuts, toasted and smashed

2 tablespoons tamarind paste

1/4 cup (60 mL) fresh lemon juice

1 tablespoon sugar

2 tablespoons fish sauce

2 cloves garlic, peeled and minced

2 Thai chilis, minced, plus more to taste

PREPARATION

1. Make the salad: Combine the green papaya, carrot, French beans, cherry tomatoes and peanuts in a bowl.

2. Make the dressing: In a small bowl, whisk together the tamarind paste, lemon juice, sugar, fish sauce, garlic, and chilis.

3. Construct: Pour the dressing over the fruits and vegetables. Toss gently to thoroughly coat everything in the dressing. Let the salad sit for 5-10 minutes, then serve.

Misono

Chef Song is a man of many laughs. There's the gleeful giggle that bursts out when he talks about the time he caught a 38 kilogram tuna off the coast of Mombasa. (Apparently he was so sore afterwards that he could barely drive his manual car home. He demonstrated the face his wife made when he tried to drive with the seat all fully reclined). There's the twinkling smile that accompanies a story of the first time he tasted kobe beef sashimi as a young chef, which involved sneaking into a walk-in fridge while everyone else was out at lunch and slicing off a piece (or two, or three.) There's the mischievous belly laugh that interrupted his recounting of the time he prepared panda paw with Parma ham and shark fin for the head of the Safari Club in Seoul, where he worked in the French restaurant. Instead of serving the powerful left paw as instructed, he secretly switched it out with the weaker right and ate the left himself. Then there's the satisfied chuckle when he talks about how, whenever he sees good steaks at the market, he'll buy the whole lot so he can enjoy them with his nightly half bottle of red wine. Finally, there's the proud grin when he describes how he goes to his restaurant on Sundays when it's closed to prepare enough food to feed all 200 members of his church.

Mr. Song grew up in Seoul, Korea. Unsure about what to do after graduation from high school, he took a job as a dishwasher at the Yoosum Club, which was located within the US Embassy and was the oldest French restaurant in Korea. With this stroke of luck, Chef Song began his love affair with restaurants and food.

After three months as a dishwasher at the Yoosum Club, he was promoted to prep cook after winning a potato peeling contest against cooks from seven other French restaurants in the city. Just three months later, when former Vice President George H.W. Bush praised Mr. Song's cream of broccoli soup, he was promoted to sous chef.

After almost five years, Mr. Song moved on to learning Japanese cuisine, first in the Japanese restaurant of the Korea Safari Club, and then in exclusive restaurants in Japan. When a member of the Korea Safari Club decided to move to Kenya to open a hotel, he offered Chef Song the opportunity to move to Nairobi to manage the Asian cuisine in the hotel's seven restaurants. Intending to stay for two years to learn English and see the continent, Chef Song left behind his wife and one year-old son. He arrived in Kenya via Hong Kong and Bombay with eighty dollars, the clothes on his back, and his knives. Within three months he sent for his family, having fallen in love with the country. After trying to quit three times over the course of eight and a half years, he finally left the Safari Club to open his own restaurant, Misono, in April 1995.

Today, he's still a permanent fixture at his restaurant, cooking daily and taking a break every day at 4:00 pm to hit nine holes of golf with his wife before returning for dinner service. Every two weeks they travel to Mombasa to check in on their restaurant there, and despite the heat he still jumps behind the counter and cooks.

The best way to describe Chef Song is the way he describes himself: as an eating professional who is always happy. If you're eating his food and talking to him, it's impossible not to feel happy, too.

~~~ HAN DI YUAN ~~~

CUCUMBER COLD DISH

 SERVES
6

This dish is intensely spicy, sour, and just a little sweet - in other words, perfect.

 TIME
Total Time: 25 minutes
Active Time: 20 minutes

INGREDIENTS
12-14 trumpet mushrooms, soaked in warm water for 30 minutes
15 tofu skins, cut into strips and soaked in warm water for 30 minutes
1/4 cup (60 mL) Chinese black vinegar
2 small hot peppers, minced
1 tablespoon white sugar
1 teaspoon salt
1 cucumber, quartered and cut into slices
3 green onions, finely chopped
1/4 cup (35 grams) crushed peanuts
1/4 cup (20 grams) chopped fresh cilantro
2 tablespoons toasted sesame seeds

 PREPARATION

1. Prepare the mushrooms & tofu skins: Bring two medium pots of water (or vegetable broth) to a boil. Add the trumpet mushrooms to one and the tofu skins to the other. Let the mushrooms simmer for about 20 minutes; simmer the tofu skins simmer for 10-15 minutes, until they are tender. Strain both the tofu skins and the mushrooms and set them aside.

2. Make the dressing: In a small bowl, combine the vinegar, hot peppers, sugar, and salt. Stir until the sugar and salt dissolve.

3. Put it together: In a large bowl, toss the cucumber and green onions with the tofu skins, mushrooms, peanuts, and cilantro. Pour the dressing over the salad and toss to combine.

4. Garnish: Sprinkle sesame seeds over the salad and serve.

NOTES

If you can't find tofu skins, you can use firm tofu in a pinch. Drain the liquid from a block of tofu (about 10 ounces / 285 grams) and press the block between two layers of paper towel or clean kitchen towels to remove excess moisture. Then, slice the tofu into thin strips and mix with the other salad ingredients.

~ MAMA ASHANTI ~

NIGERIAN PEPPER SOUP

SERVES
6-8

This soup is accurately named: it is a spicy, peppery dish that will quickly clear your sinuses. If you don't have a slow cooker, you can cook it in a Dutch oven or a large pot with a heavy lid, so long as you're sure to keep the heat very low.

TIME
Total Time: 4 hours
Active Time: 20 minutes

SPECIAL TOOLS
Slow Cooker or Dutch oven

INGREDIENTS FOR THE MARINADE

2 1/4 pounds (1 kg) goat meat (or mutton), cubed
3 medium yellow onions, minced
2 1/2 tablespoons minced ginger
1 tablespoon ground pepper (for a less peppery soup, use 1/2 tablespoon)
1 teaspoon salt

FOR THE SPICE MIX

1/2 teaspoon coriander powder
1/2 teaspoon cumin powder
1/2 teaspoon ginger powder
1/2 teaspoon ground cloves
1/4 teaspoon ground nutmeg
1/4 teaspoon ground cinnamon
Pinch of red pepperflakes or cayenne pepper

FOR THE SOUP

3 medium tomatoes, roughly chopped
2 medium yellow onions, sliced
4 cups (1 litre) water, plus more as needed
Handful of chopped basil, to garnish

PREPARATION

1. Marinate the meat: Combine the onions, ginger, pepper and one teaspoon salt in a blender or food processor. Blend until you have a smooth paste. Place the cubed meat in a large bowl and pour the marinade over. Allow the meat to marinate for at least 30 minutes.

2. Make the spice mix: In a small bowl, stir together all of the spices.

3. Slow cook: Place the meat, along with all of its marinade, in the bowl of a slow cooker. Sprinkle the tomatoes, onions, and the spices over. Add enough water to cover the meat and vegetables, then add another inch of water (about 1 liter in total, but more or less depending on the dimensions of your slow cooker). Turn the cooker on low heat and allow the stew to cook for 3-4 hours, until the meat is very tender. Taste; add salt as needed.

4. Serve: Serve the soup with a handful of finely chopped basil.

~~~ LA SALUMERIA ~~~

LA TAGLIATA

SERVES
2

La Salumeria cuts the beef in this dish before grilling, which is a simple bit of genius: it means that you can control the cooking time of all parts of the filet. Large strips from the center of the cut will need the full cooking time, but don't hesitate to remove the smaller pieces from the ends a bit earlier.

TIME
Total Time: 20 minutes
Active Time: 20 minutes

PREPARATION

1. Prepare the meat: Sprinkle 1-2 teaspoon of salt over the beef filet. Then, cut it against the grain into 1/2-inch thick slices.

2. Cook the beef: Heat the olive oil in a large skillet. When the oil is very hot, add the sliced beef. Cook 2 minutes on one side, then turn and cook 2 minutes on the other. Remove the meat from the pan and let it rest on a plate.

3. Make the sauce: Add the garlic and rosemary to the pan and cook for one minute, until the garlic begins to brown. Add 3/4 cup water and use a whisk to pull the meat drippings, garlic, and rosemary into a thin sauce. Cook about 5 minutes, just until it begins to thicken.

4. Plate: Massage the arugula with a tablespoon of olive oil. Place a handful of arugula in the middle of two plates. Place the strips of beef atop the arugula and drizzle the pan sauce over. Top with the parmesan shavings and a few grinds of black pepper, if desired.

INGREDIENTS

1 9-ounce (250-gram) beef fillet
1-2 teaspoons salt
2 tablespoons olive oil, for cooking
5 cloves garlic, minced
1 sprig fresh rosemary, leaves removed and roughly chopped
3/4 cup (180 mL) water
Handful of arugula
1 tablespoon olive oil, for the salad
6-8 pieces of shaved parmesan
Salt and pepper, to taste

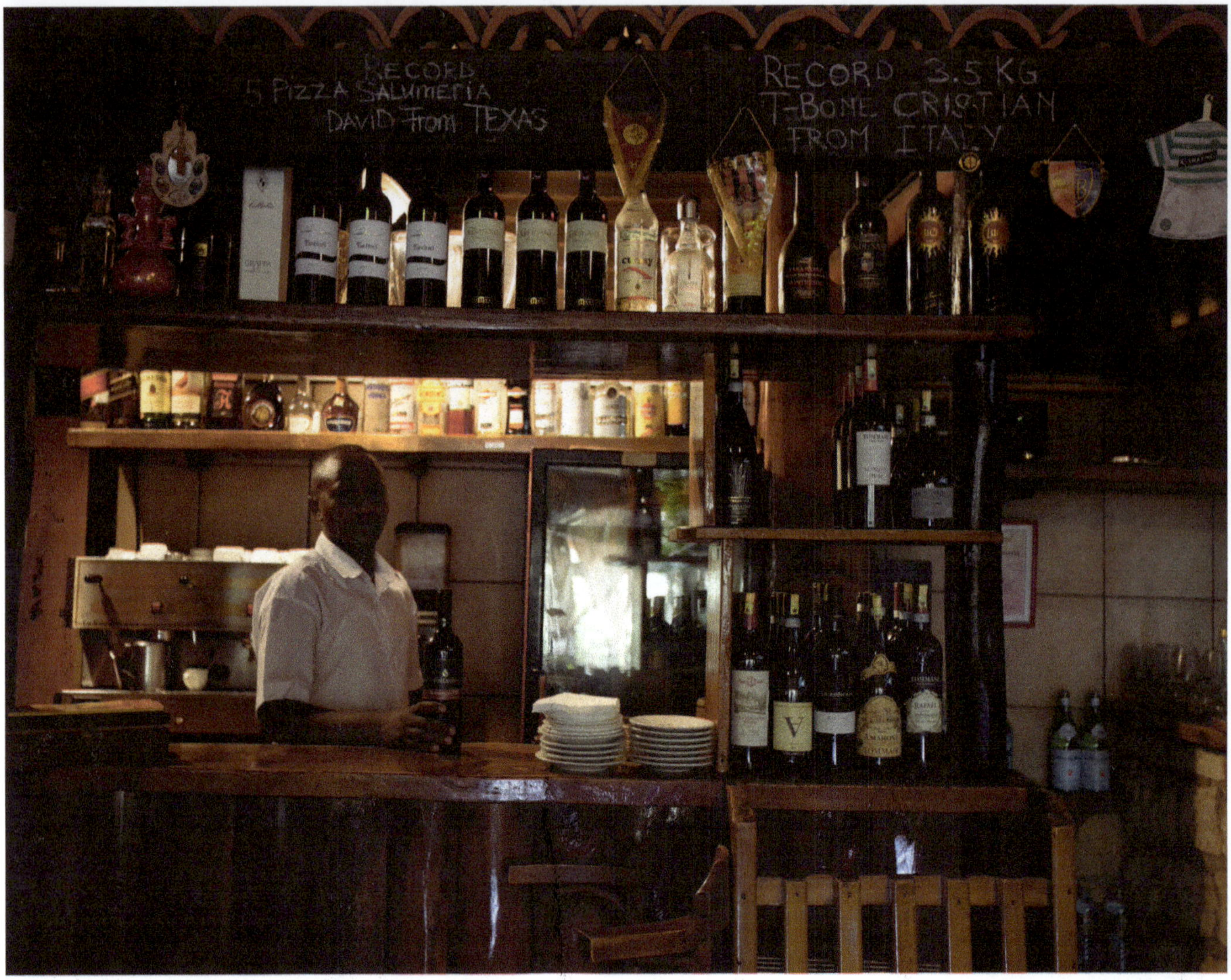
RECORD
5 PIZZA SALUMERIA
DAVID From TEXAS
RECORD 3.5 KG
T-BONE CRISTIAN
FROM ITALY

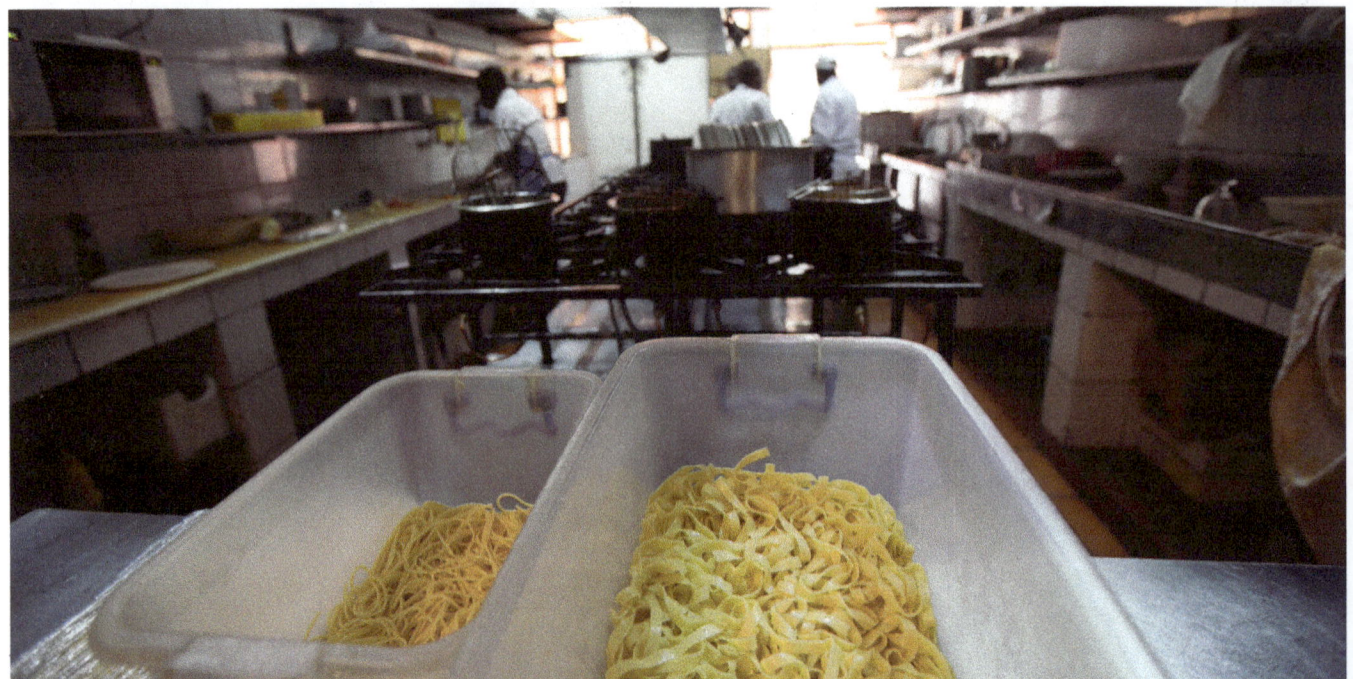

La Salumeria

Today, La Salumeria is an adored Italian institution, but opening an Italian restaurant was never Davide Buranello's plan. A dental technician by training, he spent three years in the Seychelles before coming to Nairobi in 1991 to visit some friends. He took up the import business, providing Nairobians with luxury porcelain bathtubs, sinks, and tile from Italy. By the late 1990s, however, business had slumped, and Davide found himself in Nairobi with a lot of time on his hands.

"So I started a little sandwich bar," he said. "You know, the counter, the pasta, bla bla bla. I had seven tables and fourteen benches. Then the cowboys"—he means so-called Kenyan cowboys, immigrants from the United Kingdom with roots in Kenya dating back to the colonial era —"got fed up with pasta, so I added steaks."

La Salumeria's steaks are serious. One patron once ate a 3.5 kilogram (that's almost 8 pounds) helping, setting a longstanding record. When Davide tried to congratulate the man with some tiramisu on the house, "The guy told me to go to hell," he said with a laugh. Alongside the plaque commemorating that feat are shelves and shelves of award-winning Italian wines, grappa, and limoncello. But, as it turns out, Davide doesn't drink wine. "My father was a connoisseur," he told us, "But I just don't have the taste for it."

Davide is modest about the delicious food that La Salumeria serves. "Every Italian knows more or less how to cook from the time they spend with momma," he said, but the essential factor for him is time.

When asked about how he's managed to hire and retain a skilled staff, many of whom have been at the restaurant for a decade or more, he said that everyone starts out cleaning the bathrooms. The ones who are committed stick around until they're cleaning the dining area, then making salads. At that point, Davide really commits to training them in traditional Italian cooking. As we chatted, one chef rolled out enormous sheets of homemade pasta in the kitchen, dolloping them with a mixture of spinach and ricotta and folding them expertly into ravioli. "Yeah," Davide said, glancing into the kitchen, "He's been here about 10 years."

At this point, the power went out, throwing us into darkness and the kitchen into quiet. Davide sighed. "This is the challenge. You have to improvise all the time. But you live with the problems." Then the back-up generator kicked in, the lights flickered on, and the refrigerators hummed back to life.

MONIKO'S

SPICY CALAMARI SALAD

SERVES
4

We love this salad because it doesn't shy away from a little bitterness, perhaps the least appreciated of the five tastes. If you find arugula to be too spicy, replace it with additional salad greens.

TIME
Total Time: 40 minutes
Active Time: 40 minutes

INGREDIENTS FOR THE CALAMARI

1/4 cup (60 mL) lemon juice
3 tablespoons fish sauce
2 teaspoons brown sugar
1 teaspoon minced garlic
Pinch of chili flakes
2 tablespoons finely chopped cilantro
2 tablespoons finely chopped basil
12 ounces (340 grams) cleaned calamari rings
A little neutral oil, for grilling

FOR THE GRAPEFRUIT VINAIGRETTE

1/4 cup (60 mL) grapefruit juice
1 teaspoon white wine vinegar
1 teaspoon honey
6 tablespoons olive oil
1/2 teaspoon salt

FOR THE SALAD

2 packed cups (about 100 grams) arugula
2 packed cups (about 150 grams) mixed lettuce greens
Zest of 1 lemon
1 small head of fennel, cleaned and very thinly sliced
1 small bunch of parsley, finely chopped
1 grapefruit, peeled and broken into segments

PREPARATION

1. Marinate the calamari: In a medium bowl, combine the lemon juice, fish sauce, brown sugar, garlic, chili flakes, cilantro, and basil. Whisk to combine, then add the calamari rings. Let the calamari marinate for at least 30 minutes, or for up to 4 hours.

2. Make the vinaigrette: In a small bowl or jar, combine the grapefruit juice, white wine vinegar, honey, olive oil, and salt. Whisk thoroughly to combine. Set the dressing aside.

3. Grill the calamari: Heat a little neutral oil in a large pan over very high heat. Use a slotted spoon to remove the calamari from its marinade and gently pat it dry with a paper towel. When the oil is very hot, add the calamari and cook for one minute on each side. (Don't cook the calamari for any more than two minutes, or it will be rubbery.)

4. Build the salad: Place the arugula, lettuce, lemon zest, sliced fennel, parsley, and grapefruit segments in a large bowl. Pour the vinaigrette over the salad fixings and toss to coat. Sprinkle the calamari rings over.

5. Serve: Serve the salad on its own, or together with grilled bread.

NOTES

For a particularly beautiful plating, you can supreme the grapefruit instead of simply peeling it. To do so, cut off the top and bottom of the grapefruit so that it sits flat on a cutting board. Use a sharp knife to cut away the pith and peel from top to bottom. After removing the peel, use your knife to cut the grapefruit segments apart by slicing vertically on each side of the white membranes.

Sides

82	SOMALI RICE	Al Yusra
86	FAROFA	Fogo Gaucho
88	JOLLOF RICE	Mama Ashanti
90	SPECIAL GARLIC CHIPS	Chowpaty
94	RICE AND PEAS	Taste of Jamaica
96	KIMCHI FRIED RICE	Han Di Yuan

~~~ AL YUSRA ~~~

SOMALI RICE

 **SERVES**
6-8

This dish goes above and beyond a typical rice side dish: it is rich, creamy, and amazingly flavorful. If you prefer not to have whole spices in your rice, you can tie them up in a piece of cheesecloth secured with kitchen twine. If you do that, simply add the spice bag at the same time as the water. You'll lose some of the spices' aroma but still benefit from their flavor.

 TIME
Total Time: 30 minutes
Active Time: 20 minutes

 INGREDIENTS

2 tablespoons olive oil
2 medium white onions, diced
6 cloves garlic, minced
3-4 whole cinnamon sticks
1 tablespoon cardamom pods
1/2 tablespoon cumin seeds
4-5 beef marrow bones
2 cups (480 ml) water
1 teaspoon salt, plus more to taste
2 cups (480 ml) whole cow or camel milk
3 cups (600 grams) uncooked white rice
4 tablespoons (80 grams) ghee

 PREPARATION

1. Toast the spices: In a large skillet or a medium pot, heat the olive oil over medium heat. Add the onions and garlic and cook for 2-3 minutes. Add the cinnamon sticks, cardamom pods, and cumin seeds and let them toast for about 3 minutes; they should be quite aromatic. Add the marrow bones, 2 cups of water, and the salt.

2. Cook the rice: When the water comes to a boil, add the milk. Allow the liquid to again come to a boil, then add the rice. Stir gently to combine, then add the ghee tablespoon by tablespoon, stirring well after each addition. Reduce the heat to low.

3. Let the rice cook, uncovered, for 10-12 minutes, until the surface is looking dry. Then, reduce the heat to low, cover the pan with a lid, and cook for two more minutes. Turn off the heat and let the rice rest, covered, for 5 minutes more.

4. Use a small spoon to scoop the marrow out of the bones; discard the bones (or set them aside to make stock later). Stir the marrow thoroughly into the rice. Taste and add salt as needed.

5. Serve: Serve as a side to meat, or whenever you would use plain rice.

Furusato

As a child, Mr. Lee loved maps; he loved dreaming of someday seeing the world. When his brother and sister both moved to Nairobi, he decided to leave Korea and come along, too. They were working at the Safari Park Hotel, the same hotel that Chef Song of Misono came to work for a decade before. Coincidentally, after a few years of importing food and goods from Korea, Mr. Lee succeeded Chef Song at the hotel. Nairobi may be a big city, but it can often feel like a small town.

In 2001, Mr. Lee decided to open Furusato with his wife, who is Japanese. Despite being Korean, Mr. Lee grew up eating Japanese food, and his wife, who is trained in Japanese cuisine, taught their staff how to make sushi and other Japanese foods. They started out in a small location behind Sarit Centre in the heart of Westlands, and then eight years ago moved to their current location, which they built from the ground up. They now employ fifty-two staff, six of whom have worked at Furusato from day one. Two of their staff are Filipino sushi chefs who they recruited from Dubai to manage the sushi-making operations.

Furusato means hometown in Japanese, Korean and Chinese. Mr. Lee explained that he decided on this name because he wants his customers to feel like they're at home. This sentiment is especially poignant since so many of the restaurants that we've featured have names that allude to home in some way. It seems that this desire to welcome a customer home must have something to do with these restaurants' long lasting success. Mr. Lee, like so many of these restaurateurs, has prioritized the happiness and well-being of his customers above all. While they've made what seem to be comfortable livings from their work, it's evident that they're not in it for the money; they love what they do and they care. Their customers are their family. They celebrate their joys and share their sorrows.

For immigrants so far from home, the definitions of family and home take on different meanings. Family is intentionally created: you build it with the people you choose to surround yourself with, rely on, and care for. Home is both where you are and someplace far away. Mr. Lee has created a home in Nairobi for himself, his family, and his customers.

s̄

FOGO GAUCHO

FAROFA

SERVES
4

This classic Brazilian side dish is a perfect accompaniment to grilled meat, but it also makes a wonderful stand in for rice or couscous. It soaks up juices beautifully.

TIME
Total Time: 30 minutes
Active Time: 30 minutes

INGREDIENTS
4 tablespoons butter, divided
1 yellow onion, chopped
2 cups (245 grams) cassava flour (also called gari or manioc)
2 tablespoons chopped parsley
1/2 teaspoon salt, plus more to taste
1/2 teaspoon salt

PREPARATION

1. In a medium pan over medium heat, melt 2 tablespoons of the butter. Sauté the onions in the butter until golden brown, 7-10 minutes. Reduce the heat to very low and add the remaining 2 tablespoons butter. Stir to melt, then add the cassava flour. Continue cooking on the heat for one minute, then remove from the heat and continue stirring until the cassava flour is golden and has a toasty smell.

2. Season: Stir in the parsley and salt. Taste; add more salt as needed.

3. Serve: Serve farofa hot or cold as an accompaniment to meat or stews.

― MAMA ASHANTI ―

JOLLOF RICE

SERVES
6-8

Mama Ashanti makes its jollof rice with generous quantities of vegetables and chicken. Their version makes an excellent standalone dinner or a nice replacement for plain rice as an accompaniment to soups, stews, or curries.

TIME
Total Time: 1 hour
Active Time: 1.5 hours

INGREDIENTS
1 tablespoon neutral oil
2 medium yellow onions, chopped
6 medium tomatoes, chopped
2 teaspoons salt, plus more to taste
2 teaspoons curry powder
2 medium carrots, peeled and cut into very small cubes
7 ounces (200 grams) French beans, ends removed and quartered
¼ head of green cabbage, grated or finely chopped
3 cups (510 grams) cooked white rice (from about 2 cups dry rice)
2 chicken breasts

PREPARATION

1. Cook the sauce: In a medium pot, heat the oil over medium heat. Add the onions and cook for 2-3 minutes, stirring, until they are translucent. Add the tomatoes, salt, and curry powder and cook, stirring occasionally, until the tomatoes start to break down, about 10 minutes. Add the carrots, French beans, and cabbage. Reduce the heat to low and simmer until the vegetables are al dente, about 10 minutes more.

2. Poach the chicken: While the sauce is simmering, prepare a small pot of lightly salted boiling water. Cut the chicken into very small pieces and boil it for 2-3 minutes, until each piece is cooked through. Strain the chicken out of the cooking water and set the chicken aside.

3. Combine: Add the rice and the cooked chicken to the tomato sauce. Stir well to coat the rice in the sauce. Cook for 2-3 minutes to rewarm the rice and the chicken. Taste; add salt as needed.

4. Serve: Enjoy jollof rice by itself or served together with a stew.

NOTES
You can easily make this dish vegetarian by removing the chicken. If you do so, consider upping the quantity of carrots, French beans, and cabbage by about 25%.

~~~ CHOWPATY ~~~

SPECIAL GARLIC CHIPS

 **SERVES**
4-6, as an appetizer

Created in response to Kenyan customers' frequent requests, Chowpaty's special garlic chips have become legendary in Nairobi. This homemade version bakes the potatoes rather than deep-frying them, and the result is *this close* to being as delicious as the real thing.

 TIME
Total Time: 45 minutes - 1 hour
Active Time: 20 minutes

 INGREDIENTS
10 large potatoes (about 2 pounds/1 kg), peeled and cut into French fry-sized pieces
4 tablespoons (60 mL) oil
1 head garlic, peeled and very finely minced
1/2 tablespoon chilli powder
1/2 tablespoon curry powder
2 teaspoons salt, plus more to taste
1 tablespoon white vinegar
2 limes, quartered

 PREPARATION

1. Preheat the oven: Turn the oven to 425F (220C). Place a large ungreased baking tray or cast iron pan, if you have one, in the oven to preheat.

2. Prep the potatoes: In a large bowl, toss the potatoes with the oil. Add the garlic, chilli powder, curry powder, and salt.

3. Bake: Carefully transfer the potatoes to the preheated pan. Bake for 10 minutes, then stir; bake for another 10 minutes. The potatoes should be golden and tender when poked with a fork. If they're not yet golden, bake for up to 15 minutes more. Remove the fries from the oven and let them cool for 10 minutes on a paper towel-lined tray. Try a fry and add salt and chili to taste.

4. Serve: Transfer the fries to a serving dish and sprinkle them with vinegar. Serve with the lime wedges.

NOTES

1. An entire head of garlic may seem like a lot, but trust Chowpaty on this one. Garlic is key for these fries.

2. Not all chilli powders are created equal. If you worry that a half tablespoon of the variety you have on hand will make the fries punishingly hot, then reduce the amount according to your instinct. You can always shake extra chilli powder over the fries once they come out of the oven.

Table 49

We started this series with Christian, who closed his restaurant at the Alliance Française in 1991 to join Alan Bobbe, his mentor and Nairobi's premier French chef. For twelve years the Jardin du Paris sat empty, until 2003, when the French Ambassador invited Daniel Lienard to revive the beloved restaurant. In some ways it was a passing of the torch from one French chef to another, and Daniel honored the cuisine by serving classical French food in the heart of Nairobi's central business district for twelve years.

Daniel first came to Kenya on holiday with his family, escaping Paris and the two restaurants that he owned there. His friend had a house on the coast, and Daniel had planned to stay for a month to relax with his wife and young children. That short holiday slowly became an indefinite stay. They moved to Kilifi, a town on the Kenyan coast, and for ten years he operated a guesthouse and taught scuba diving. They then moved farther north to the island of Kiwayu, where he stayed for a decade before moving to Nairobi to work for the Governor's Camp, a luxury safari lodge group. After a decade that included managing the opening of a lodge in Rwanda for gorilla trekkers, he decided to take the French ambassador's offer and start a restaurant.

Given his formal culinary training, which included two years as a pastry chef, Daniel developed a classically French menu for the restaurant. He would buy whole pigs and butcher them himself, making use of all parts of the animal, turning them into pâté, boudin noir, and other delectables. He found a farmer raising ducks in nearby Naivasha that he would confit, rabbits he would braise, and even taught his eleven staff how to bake fresh bread and make croissants and other pastries from scratch. Despite being thousands of miles from France, the food was wholly authentic.

In 2013, the restaurant changed hands again, this time to a French company that operates airport cafes. Perhaps it's a sign of the times, the fast-changing economy reflecting new tastes and lifestyles. Now, none of the food is prepared in the restaurant and it seems that, at least for the time being, the long legacy of Nairobi's authentic downtown French restaurants has ended.

―― HAN DI YUAN ――

KIMCHI FRIED RICE

 SERVES
6

Han Di Yuan's kimchi fried rice can be an impressive side dish or a main in its own right. To make it vegetarian, simply omit the sausage. If you wish, you can swap in firm tofu in its place.

TIME
Total Time: 15 minutes
Active Time: 25 minutes

 PREPARATION

1. Cook the eggs, vegetables, and meat: Heat the oil in a wide, flat pan over high heat. Beat the eggs lightly in a bowl and add them to the pan. When the eggs begin to solidify, add the carrot and cucumber. Reduce the heat to medium and add the sausage and kimchi. Stir to combine, then cover with a lid. Remove the lid and stir every 3-4 minutes to ensure it's not sticking to the pan. After 10 minutes, test one of the carrot pieces; continue to cook until the carrots are tender, up to 10 minutes more.

2. Add the rice: When the carrots are soft and the sausage is cooked, add the cooked rice and soy sauce and stir thoroughly to combine. Cook another 2-3 minutes, just until the rice is warmed through and well coated. Taste; add salt or soy sauce as needed.

 INGREDIENTS

¼ cup (60 mL) neutral oil

6 eggs

2 large carrots, peeled and cut into very small cubes

1 cucumber, cut into very small cubes

6 links (about 8 ounces / 250 grams) Chinese sausage, cut into small pieces

2 cups (400 grams) prepared kimchi, roughly chopped

3 cups (510 grams) cooked white rice

2 tablespoons soy sauce, plus more to taste

Salt, to taste

~~~ TASTE OF JAMAICA ~~~

RICE AND PEAS

 SERVES
6

For those who are not from either the American South or Jamaica, it might seem odd that there are no peas in this recipe. Rather, peas refers to kidney beans.

 TIME
Total Time: 30 minutes
Active Time: 15 minutes

 INGREDIENTS
2 tablespoons neutral oil
6 cloves garlic, peeled and minced
6 green onions, chopped, plus more to garnish
3 teaspoons dried thyme
¾ cup (165 mL) coconut milk
1 tablespoon butter
2 cups (400 grams) uncooked white rice
3 ½ cups (840 mL) water
Half a hot pepper, left intact
2 teaspoons salt
2 cups (340 grams) cooked kidney beans

 PREPARATION

1. **Prepare the cooking liquid:** In a large pan, heat the oil over medium-high heat. Add the garlic and cook until it just starts to brown. Add the green onions and the thyme and stir to coat them with the oil. Add the coconut milk and the butter and bring to a simmer.

2. **Cook the rice:** Add the rice and stir well to coat. Add the water, hot pepper, and salt and simmer, uncovered, for 15 minutes, until the liquid is absorbed and the rice is al dente. Add the beans, stir, and turn off the heat. Remove the hot pepper. Taste; add salt as needed.

3. **Serve:** Serve with a sprinkle of chopped green onions, as an accompaniment to dishes like jerk chicken (page 136).

"Find the best ingredients, prepare them simply, don't waste, and everything will be okay."

Seth, Marula Mercantile

Vegetarian Mains

100	YAKI UDON	Misono
102	AVOCADO URAMAKI	Misono
106	PASTA SALDATO	Al Yusra
108	MAPO TOFU	Chengdu Impressions
110	INJERA	Ethiopian
112	SHRO WAT	Ethiopian
113	SPICY LENTILS	Ethiopian
114	VEGETARIAN PLATTER	Ethiopian
118	PANEER TIKKA MASALA	Chowpaty
120	FALAFEL	D'Afric
122	ASIAN SLAW	Juniper Social
126	RAVIOLI WITH RICOTTA AND SPINACH	La Salumeria
128	GARLIC BUTTER MASALA DOSA	Chowpaty

— MISONO —

YAKI UDON (VEGETARIAN FRIED NOODLES)

SERVES
About 4

Chef Song gives these words to the wise: make sure your noodles are ready at the same time your vegetables are. The worst thing, he says, is to end up with overcooked vegetables because you were waiting for noodles to cook. Better to have the noodles cooked, drained and on hand and then allow them to rewarm in the wok.

TIME
Total Time: 30 minutes
Active Time: 30 minutes

INGREDIENTS FOR THE SAUCE

4 tablespoons soy sauce
1 teaspoon tomato paste
1 teaspoon smooth Dijon mustard
1 teaspoon honey
1 teaspoon minced ginger
1 tablespoon mirin
2 tablespoons soy sauce
2 tablespoons water

FOR THE STIR FRY

250 grams dried udon noodles (or 400 grams fresh)
6 tablespoons neutral oil, divided
2 heads broccoli, broken into small florets
8-12 stalks of asparagus, cut into small pieces
6 small eggplants (or 2 large ones), cubed
4 cloves garlic, peeled and roughly chopped
4-5 baby bok choy, roughly chopped

TO FINISH

1 tablespoon butter
2 tablespoons neutral oil
2 tablespoons mirin

PREPARATION

1. Cook the noodles: If your noodles aren't fresh, bring a large pot of lightly salted water to a boil. Add the noodles and cook until they are al dente, about 6 minutes. Rinse in cold water and set the noodles aside.

2. Make the sauce: In a small bowl, combine the soy sauce, tomato paste, mustard, honey, ginger, mirin, soy sauce, and water. Stir well to combine. Set aside.

3. Fry the vegetables: Heat 2 tablespoons oil in a large wok over high heat. When the oil begins to smoke, add the broccoli and cook, without stirring, for two minutes. Flip the florets and cook another 2 minutes; they should be nicely browned all over. Add 2 more tablespoons of oil to the pan, then add the asparagus and the eggplant and cook until the flesh of the eggplant is golden, about 5 minutes more.

4. Add the garlic and the bok choy and cook, stirring, for 2-3 minutes, until the bok choy is wilted and has released its moisture.

5. Deglaze: Add the sauce to the pan and stir to coat the vegetables and pull up any stuck-on bits from the bottom of the pan. Add the noodles. Stir well to coat the noodles with the sauce and cook until the noodles are thoroughly heated.

6. Finish: Add a tablespoon of butter, 2 tablespoons oil, and two tablespoons of mirin to the noodles. Stir to melt the butter. Garnish with spring onions and serve very hot.

NOTES

You can use a different selection of vegetables, depending on the season and availability. Feel free to try white cabbage, sugar snap peas, or zucchini in place of the vegetables listed above. When frying, just make sure to go from hardest vegetable to softest.

~ MISONO ~

AVOCADO URAMAKI

 **MAKES**
3 Maki Rolls

The quality of your avocado is key to this recipe. If all you can find are rock hard avocados, let them ripen in a paper bag for a day or two. You'll be glad you did.

 TIME
Total Time: 40 minutes
Active Time: 40 minutes

 INGREDIENTS FOR THE SUSHI RICE

1 cup (200 grams) uncooked sushi rice
1 1/4 cups (300 mL) water
1/3 cup (80 mL) rice vinegar
2 tablespoons sugar
1/2 teaspoon salt

FOR THE ASPARAGUS TEMPURA

6-9 pieces of asparagus
1/2 cup (120 mL) cold water
1/2 cup (65 grams) white flour
1 egg yolk
1/4 teaspoon baking soda
1/2 teaspoon salt
1/4 cup neutral oil

FOR THE SUSHI

3 pieces nori (sushi seaweed)
2 cups cooked sushi rice
3 tablespoons sesame seeds (white or black)
6-9 pieces asparagus tempura
1 medium avocado
2 tablespoons soy sauce
Soy sauce for dipping
Wasabi and pickled ginger, to serve

 PREPARATION

1. Make the sushi rice: Thoroughly rinse the sushi rice, then place it in a medium pot and cover with the water. Cook, uncovered, until the water has evaporated and the rice is al dente. While the rice is still hot, stir in the rice vinegar, sugar, and salt and allow the rice to cool.

2. Make the asparagus tempura: In a medium bowl, whisk together the water, flour, egg yolk, baking soda, and salt. Heat the oil in a medium pan over high heat. Trim the fibrous ends off the asparagus, then dip each piece of asparagus into the tempura batter and carefully place it into the hot oil. Cook, turning if needed, until the tempura is golden on all sides, 5-7 minutes in total. Turn off the heat and place the cooked asparagus onto a paper towel-lined plate.

3. Prepare the sushi rice & seaweed: Place a piece of cling film on a large cutting board. Place a piece of nori on the plastic and spread one-third of your rice over it, pressing down hard to compact the rice. Sprinkle sesame seeds over and press them into the rice. Place another piece of cling film over the rice and carefully flip the whole thing over so that the rice is now on the bottom. Set the cutting board aside.

4. Construct: Place 2-3 pieces of asparagus tempura at the top edge of the nori. Carefully roll up the nori, using the cling film to apply pressure as you do so. When you come to the bottom, lightly brush the nori with water and press to seal. Repeat with the remaining nori, rice, sesame seeds, and asparagus.

5. Prepare the avocado: Cut the avocado in half, remove the pit, and cut the meat into slices. Cut each slice in half. Place the slices atop the maki rolls, pressing down to adhere them to the rice.

6. Cut: Place the rolls on a cutting board. Using a very sharp knife, cut each roll into 8-10 even pieces.

7. Garnish: Drizzle the sushi with a little soy sauce.

8. Serve: Serve the maki with a small bowl of soy sauce for dipping and wasabi and pickled ginger, if available.

NOTES

When choosing your asparagus, select thin stalks: they will be easier to bite through.

Al Yusra

The story of Al-Yusra starts in the 1970s, 1300 kilometers outside of Nairobi in the dusty, dry deserts of Northern Kenya. Bakai Maalim Kulmia was one of twenty-five children of a pastoralist camel herder. His father owned over two thousand camels, and whenever the family was in need of food or goods, he would send one or two of his sons to nearby Elwak town to sell the camels for cash and shop for the family. When Bakai was a teenager, his turn finally came to go to the market for the first time. Awed by the town and the lifestyle of its people, instead of selling the camels and buying food, Bakai and a brother who accompanied him decided to run away with the money. They took the cash, which wasn't an insignificant amount (today, a single adult camel can retail between 800 and 1000 USD), and opened a shop in the town, where they would resell products they'd bought across the border in Somalia for a profit. His family knew what he was doing--his father would send people to check in on him--but he wasn't allowed to return home until he'd repaid his father the money he'd stolen. Within a year, they'd earned enough money to repay their father, and within the decade, he and his brother moved to Nairobi together to open a shop in Eastleigh, a predominantly Somali neighborhood in the heart of the city. Along with three other partners, they grew the business into a hugely successful regional wholesaler of fast-moving consumer goods. By the 1990s, they were millionaires.

In 2005, the group decided to open a restaurant. They'd identified a market opening for Somali food in the central business district and found a location adjacent to Jamia Mosque, Nairobi's largest mosque. The mosque was built in 1925 and has capacity for 20,000 people, about 80% of whom are Somali. Each day during the call to prayer, you can see people streaming towards the mosque and then to Al Yusra. Bakai's son, Abdi, boasted that you could order a tea at Al Yusra, drink some, head to the mosque for prayers, and it'd still be warm when you returned.

Abdul Wahab, one of Bakai's nineteen children, now manages the restaurant with his brother Abdi. When he and his siblings were growing up, their father would wake them up at 5:00 am during school holidays for prayers and then send them off to work. They are proud to have their father's work ethic, and it's evident in the success of the restaurant. They are constantly adapting to customers' demands: they've added sandwiches and pizza to attract non-Somalis, and this year they added shwarma. Since 2005 they have opened locations in Mombasa and Kisumu, and they plan to continue to open a new location per year until there are branches across Kenya.

I was first introduced to Abdul and his brothers through a friend who had traveled with Bakai to Voi, a city 200 kilometers from Nairobi, to meet his camels. When his father died, the camels were split among his siblings. He inherited 800 camels, which he brought to live on his farm in Voi. Now, every Friday after work, Bakai drives alone or with his children to visit the camels, returning to Nairobi on Sunday. Each evening, 300 liters of milk are sent from the farm to the restaurant, arriving fresh in the morning to serve with tea. The farm also supplies camel meat to the restaurant, which is one of their most popular dishes.

It's important to note that Bakai and his sons are not, in fact, immigrants. They were born and raised in Kenya, but they are ethnically and culturally Somali. Despite being Kenyan citizens, Somali communities in Kenya have been long marginalized. When we started our conversation, before saying anything about the restaurant, Abdul and Abdi first laid the groundwork by explaining to me that, "Somalis are Somalis." There is no border to their culture or community. It's because of this that we have included them; like many immigrants, they are people who have made a home away from their homeland.

AL YUSRA

PASTA SALDATO

 SERVES
6-8

Al Yusra's take on a simple dish adds unexpected layers of nuanced flavors: the ginger and cilantro turn this pasta into something special.

 TIME
Total Time: 40 minutes
Active Time: 40 minutes

INGREDIENTS

3 tablespoons olive oil
6 cloves garlic, minced
1 tablespoon fresh ginger, minced
2 1/4 pounds (1 kg) fresh tomatoes, roughly chopped
2 teaspoons salt, plus more to taste
1 package (18 ounces / 500 grams) dry spaghetti noodles
7 ounces (200 grams) mozzarella cheese, grated
1/4 cup (25 grams) chopped cilantro leaves

 PREPARATION

1. Make the tomato sauce: In a large pan or wok, heat the olive oil over medium high heat. Add the garlic and ginger and cook until the garlic begins to brown, 2-3 minutes. Add the fresh tomatoes and salt and cook until the tomatoes start to fall apart, about 10 minutes. Reduce the heat to low and simmer, stirring occasionally, until the sauce thickens, about 20 minutes more. Taste and add salt as needed.

2. Cook the pasta: While the tomato sauce is simmering, bring a large pot of lightly salted water to a boil. Add the pasta and cook according to the package's instructions. (Most spaghetti will need about 8 minutes to be al dente.)

3. Combine: Put the cooked, drained pasta directly into the tomato sauce and stir well to combine. Add the mozzarella and stir until it's well incorporated. Top with a generous handful of cilantro.

4. Serve: Serve each person a generous mound of spaghetti topped with a scoop of braised goat meat (see page 62).

~ CHENGDU IMPRESSIONS ~

MAPO TOFU

 **SERVES**
2-3

The Sichuan peppercorns are essential to this dish, as they provide the difficult-to-replicate numbing sensation that defines much of Sichuan cuisine. Look for them at a Chinese grocery, where they may be labeled Prickly Ash. For the very best results, buy whole seeds, lightly toast them, and grind them yourself in a pepper mill or mortar and pestle.

 TIME
Total Time: 20 minutes
Active Time: 20 minutes

 INGREDIENTS
1 block (about 16 ounces / 450 grams) medium-soft tofu, cut into 1-inch cubes
1 ½ cups (360 mL) vegetable stock
1 tablespoon neutral oil
4 tablespoons ground pork (optional)
1 teaspoon black bean paste
1 teaspoon minced ginger
1 teaspoon minced garlic
1 teaspoon chili bean paste (dou ban jiang)
½ teaspoon + a pinch Sichuan peppercorn powder
1 teaspoon soy sauce
½ teaspoon sugar
1 teaspoon of cornstarch, dissolved in ¼ cup (60 mL) water to make a thin paste
Salt, to taste
Handful of chopped green onions
1-2 cups (170-340 grams) steamed white rice, to serve

 PREPARATION

1. Warm the tofu: In a small pot, bring the stock to a boil and gently add the tofu. Boil for about three minutes; you want the tofu to be warmed through. Use a slotted spoon to remove the tofu from the pot, reserving the remaining stock.

2. Make the sauce: In a large wok, heat a tablespoon of oil and add the ground pork. Once the pork starts to brown, add the black bean paste, ginger, garlic, chili bean paste, and ½ teaspoon Sichuan peppercorn powder. Cook, stirring, for 1-2 minutes, until it's fragrant.

3. Simmer: Turn the heat down to medium and add the reserved stock. Stir to incorporate. Gently add the tofu to the pan. Add the soy sauce, sugar, and cornstarch paste and stir gently to combine. Let everything simmer for about 10 minutes, until the sauce has thickened slightly and has a rich red color. Taste; add salt or soy sauce as needed.

4. Garnish: Sprinkle the mapo tofu with the chopped green garlic and a pinch of peppercorn powder.

5. Serve: Serve over steamed rice.

~~~ ETHIOPIAN ~~~

24 - HOUR INJERA

SERVES
6

Like sourdough bread, traditional injera is made using a carefully-tended starter, which must be developed over the course of at least 10 days and fed regularly. The version we offer here is akin to making bread with instant yeast: you'll still need a little patience, but the timeline is much more approachable.

TIME
Total Time: 24 hours
Active Time: 30 minutes

INGREDIENTS
1 cup (120 grams) teff flour
1 ½ cups (360 mL) water
½ teaspoon + 1/8 teaspoon instant yeast
¼ teaspoon sugar
½ teaspoon salt

PREPARATION

1. The day before, make the pre-ferment: In a large bowl, combine the teff flour, water, and 1/8 teaspoon yeast. Stir to combine and cover with a clean kitchen towel. Leave the pre-ferment undisturbed on the kitchen counter for at least 24 hours, or for up to 36.

2. Finish the batter: After 24 hours, the batter should have a nice sour smell. Gently whisk it to reincorporate any liquid that has risen to the top, then stir in the remaining ½ teaspoon of yeast, the sugar, and the salt. Let the batter rest, covered, for one hour.

3. Cook the injera: Heat a little oil in your largest nonstick pan; wipe with a paper towel to remove excess grease. Use a medium cup measure to pour the batter into the pan, immediately swirling the pan as you would for a crêpe. After about 30 seconds, you'll see bubbles on the surface of the batter. Resist the urge to flip; instead, cover the pan with a lid and cook for 1-2 minutes more, until the top of the injera is moist but cooked enough that it doesn't stick to your fingers. Remove the injera from the pan with a spatula and place it on a plate. Continue cooking the rest of the batter in the same way.

4. Serve: Serve injera topped with mounds of shiro wat, grilled beans, steamed potatoes & carrots, caramelized beets, and spicy lentils.

NOTES

Restaurant injera is made on a huge griddle, yielding rounds of injera that cover enormous serving platters. For home injera, we like the rounds to be about plate-sized, so that each diner can scoop vegetables, shiro wat, and other toppings onto their personal injera. Extra injera can be set on the table and used to scoop up sauces and vegetables.

~~~ ETHIOPIAN ~~~

SHIRO WAT

SERVES
4-6, when served with injera & other toppings

If you've ever been amazed by how delicious restaurant shiro wat is, you'll be even more amazed to learn how easy it is to make at home. That said, shiro may take only 10 minutes to learn, but it can easily take a lifetime to perfect. Play around with your ratios of oil, water, berbere, and shiro to find your ideal variation.

TIME
Total Time: 20 minutes
Active Time: 20 minutes

INGREDIENTS FOR THE SHIRO

1/2 cup (120 mL) oil, divided
1 3/4 cups (420 mL) water
1 tablespoon berbere spice (see below), plus more to taste
1 cup (120 grams) shiro powder (or chickpea flour)
3 medium tomatoes, puréed
1 medium yellow onion, minced
3 cloves garlic, minced

FOR THE BERBERE MIX

4 tablespoons paprika
2 teaspoons red chili powder
1 tablespoon salt
1 teaspoon ginger powder
1/2 teaspoon cardamom powder
1/2 teaspoon coriander powder
1/2 teaspoon nutmeg
1/4 teaspoon cloves
1/4 teaspoon cinnamon

PREPARATION

1. Make the berbere spice mix: In a small bowl, stir together all the ingredients. Store extra berbere, which can be used as a rub for meat, chicken, or fish, in a tightly sealed jar.

2. Make the shiro: In a medium saucepan, heat 1/4 cup (60 mL) oil. Add the onion and garlic and cook until the onion is very soft. Add the berbere and stir for a minute to toast it. Then, add the puréed tomatoes and stir for about a minute before adding in the shiro powder. Once the mixture has the consistency of a thick paste, add the water and whisk until the mixture is smooth. Add the remaining 1/4 cup of oil and cook for 5 minutes more. (The shiro should be somewhat thicker than gravy but thinner than mashed potatoes.)

3. Adjust: Taste and add more berbere, salt, water, and/or oil to bring the shiro to the spiciness and consistency you like.

4. Serve: Serve shiro atop injera. Leftovers, if there are any, can be refrigerated and used as a great alternative dip or spread with bread or vegetables.

NOTES

You can adjust the ratio of oil to water in this recipe to your liking. Restaurant shiro tends to be very oily, using closer to 1 cup (240 mL) oil and 1 1/4 cup water for 1 cup of shiro powder. We like to up the water and reduce the oil for home cooking. For even healthier—but less authentic—shiro, you can use only enough oil to cook the onions and water or vegetable stock from there on.

~ ETHIOPIAN ~

SPICY LENTILS

 SERVES

6, when served with injera & other toppings

 TIME

Total Time: 40 minutes, plus soaking time
Active Time: 20 minutes

 INGREDIENTS

1 1/2 cups (320 grams) dry red lentils

1/4 cup (60 mL) neutral oil

1 yellow onion, minced

4 cloves garlic, minced

1 tablespoon berbere spice (see page 112), plus more to taste

1/4 cup (55 grams) tomato paste

2 1/2 cups (600 mL) water

Salt, to taste

 PREPARATION

1. Soak the lentils: Place the lentils in a medium bowl and cover with warm water. Let the lentils soak for at least 2 hours or up to overnight.

2. Sauté the vegetables: Heat the oil in a medium pot over medium heat. Add the onion and garlic and cook until the onion is soft, 2-3 minutes. Add the berbere spice, tomato paste, and a generous pinch of salt and cook for one minute more. Add the lentils and stir to coat them in the tomato & spices. Then, add the water. Bring the water to a boil, then reduce the heat to a simmer.

3. Simmer: Simmer the lentils until they are tender and the water has evaporated, about 30 minutes. (If the water evaporates before the lentils are soft, add more water in 1/2 cup (120 mL) increments.) Taste; add additional salt and berbere to taste.

4. Serve: Serve lentils over injera.

~~~ ETHIOPIAN ~~~

GRILLED GREEN BEANS

 MAKES
about 2 cups

A crowd favorite at Habesha is the vegetarian platter, which consists of a massive round of injera topped with shiro wat, spicy lentils, and sides of green beans, beets, potatoes, carrots, and cabbage. If you're looking to add something green, you can also sauté kale or spinach with—you can probably guess—a dash of berbere spice.

 TIME
Total Time: 30 minutes
Active Time: 5 minutes

 PREPARATION

1. Preheat the oven to 400F (200C).

2. **Prepare the beans:** Place the green beans on a baking sheet. Drizzle oil over and toss the beans to coat thoroughly. Sprinkle them with salt and berbere.

3. **Roast:** Roast for 20-30 minutes, until the beans are very soft and have begun to blister and brown.

4. **Serve:** Serve the beans atop injera.

INGREDIENTS
2 large handfuls french beans, ends removed
About 1⁄4 cup (50 mL) neutral oil
Sprinkle of berbere spice
Salt, to taste

CARAMELIZED BEETS

 MAKES
about 2 cups

 TIME
Total Time: 45 minutes
Active Time: 10 minutes

 PREPARATION

1. Preheat the oven to 400F (200C).

2. **Make the dressing:** In a small bowl, whisk together the balsamic vinegar, oil, berbere, and salt.

3. **Roast:** Place the beets on a tin foil-lined baking sheet. Drizzle the dressing over them. Roast the beets for about 45 minutes, until they are very soft and have begun to turn golden at the edges.

4. **Serve:** Serve the beets with injera.

 INGREDIENTS
4-6 large beets, roots removed, peeled, and cut into small cubes
2 tablespoons balsamic vinegar
1⁄4 cup (60 mL) neutral oil
Sprinkle of berbere spice

~~~ ETHIOPIAN ~~~

POTATOES, CARROTS & CABBAGE (TIKIL GOMEN)

SERVES
6, when served with injera & other toppings

TIME
Total Time: 40 minutes
Active Time: 10 minutes

INGREDIENTS
3 large carrots, peeled and cut into half-moons

2 large potatoes, peeled and cut into wedges

½ head green cabbage, thinly sliced or grated

2 tablespoons neutral oil

1 cup (240 mL) water

2 teaspoons salt, plus more to taste

PREPARATION

1. Cook: Heat the oil in a large pot over medium-high heat. Add the carrots and cook until they are shiny and just beginning to turn tender, 3-5 minutes. Add the potatoes and cook 5 minutes more. Then, add the cabbage, water, and salt. Bring the water to a boil, then cover and reduce the heat to low. Simmer until all the vegetables are tender, 8-10 minutes. Taste; add salt as needed.

2. Serve: Serve tikil gomen atop injera.

Fogo Gaucho

There's no quick way to get from Brazil to Kenya. Inevitably the journey involves several legs and many hours of travel. The immense distance wasn't entirely clear to Jonny and Milton when, at twenty-four and twenty-five years old, they boarded a plane that brought them halfway around the world. Luckily, they were looking for an adventure.

Like Matthew and Anil a few blocks away at Open House, Milton and Johnny talk and act like brothers. They grew up in southern Brazil and both moved to São Paulo at a young age to work in restaurants. São Paulo invented the Brazilian churrasco style of cooking, which is essentially meat cooked on sticks over fire. Through friends they learned about the opportunity to move to Nairobi to help open a churrascuría in a new hotel. Eager to get out of Brazil and see the world, they applied together and got the job. They signed two-year contracts and before they knew it, they were professional restaurant consultants.

After their contract with the hotel expired in 2007, they decided that they wanted to stay and open a restaurant of their own. They'd seen a clear demand for the style of food they were making and wanted to try their hands at entrepreneurship. They'd saved some money and planned to start small, reinvesting everything they earned. When they started scouting for locations, they stumbled upon a small bar in an old colonial house run by an elderly woman. This crumbling house with stucco walls and terracotta roof tiles soon became a roaring temple of grilled meats.

For many Nairobians, the rules of the churrascuría were a novelty. Red and green cards are placed on the table. flip to the green side and someone magically appears with a sword stacked with delicious meat, flip to red when you're ready chow down.

When they first opened, Jonny and Milton struggled to find meat butchered and prepared in the Brazilian style. They took it upon themselves to visit a few butcheries that they liked and taught the staff how to prepare specific cuts and how to age the meat. Today, they go through 5,000 kilos of beef per month.

A few years ago they opened another location, and currently employ about one hundred people across both restaurants. They're proud that, after nearly a decade, they've trained numerous staff and have four employees who have worked with them since the beginning. When asked if they foresee themselves staying in Kenya for the long haul, both acknowledged that their family roots are now here.

"Our English is better than our Portuguese!" they exclaim.

They've found a way to pursue their passions for food and cooking, their children are growing up here, and they have their friendship. They're two gauchos in Kenya, making it work.

~~~ CHOWPATY ~~~

PANEER TIKKA MASALA

SERVES
6

Chowpaty's paneer tikka masala is a beautifully layered creation, combining three classic Indian gravies. Making all three at once requires immense kitchen coordination, so we simplify it to two for the home cook.

TIME
Total Time: 1.5 hours
Active Time: 1.5 hours

INGREDIENTS FOR THE PANEER

1 1/2 cups (340 grams) yogurt
1/2 tablespoon crushed garlic
1/2 tablespoon minced ginger
2 teaspoons cumin
1/2 teaspoon turmeric
1/2 teaspoon red chilli powder
1 teaspoon lemon juice
14 ounces (400 grams) paneer, cut into bite-sized cubes
2 small onions, sliced
1 medium sweet red pepper, seeded and cut into thin strips

FOR THE TOMATO GRAVY

3 tablespoons ghee or oil
3 medium yellow onions, diced
2 teaspoons minced ginger
2 teaspoons minced garlic
2 teaspooons garam masala spice
1/2 teaspoon chili powder
1 tablespoon coriander powder
1/2 teaspoon turmeric
1 teaspoon salt
1 teaspoon sugar
12-14 medium tomatoes, roughly chopped
1/2 cup (120 mL) water

PREPARATION: FOR THE PANEER

1. Make the marinade: Mix together the yogurt, crushed garlic, ginger, cumin, turmeric, chilli powder, and lemon juice in a large bowl.

2. Marinate:
Add the paneer, onion, and red pepper to the marinade. Stir to coat well and allow to marinade for at least one hour or up to overnight in the fridge.

FOR THE TOMATO GRAVY

1. Cook the onions & spices: Heat the ghee in a large pot over medium-high heat. Once it has melted, add the onions and cook until they begin to brown. Add the ginger and the garlic and cook for an additional minute before adding the garam masala, chili powder, coriander, turmeric, salt, and sugar. Cook for 2-3 minutes, until the spices are very aromatic and the garlic begins to brown.

2. Simmer the gravy: Add the tomatoes, pressing down on them with a spoon to break them apart. Add the water. Bring the sauce to a boil, then reduce the heat to low and allow it to simmer, stirring occasionally, until the tomatoes are completely broken down. Remove from the heat and set aside.

FOR THE WHITE GRAVY

1. First, prepare the cashews: Set the cashews aside to soak in the warm water for at least 30 minutes. Then, blend the cashews in a food processor or with a mortar and pestle. (You can also use ¾ cup smooth unsweetened cashew butter).

2. Make the sauce: Heat the ghee in a small pan over medium heat. Add the cumin, garam masala, garlic, ginger, chili, and coriander and cook for about 2 minutes. Add the cashew nut paste and stir until the spices are well incorporated; then, add the yogurt and salt and stir to combine. Let the gravy warm for 2-3 minutes, then remove from the heat.

FOR THE WHITE GRAVY

½ cup (70 grams) raw cashew nuts
½ cup (120 mL) warm water
2 teaspoons ghee
½ teaspoon cumin
1 teaspoon garam masala
½ teaspoon minced garlic
½ teaspoon ground ginger
¼ teaspoon red chili powder
½ teaspoon coriander powder
½ cup (110 mL) yogurt
½ teaspoon salt

TO FINISH

1/4 cup (20 grams) chopped cilantro
1/4 cup (65 grams) heavy cream

PUT IT ALL TOGETHER

1. Combine: Reheat the tomato gravy in a large pot. Add the paneer and all of its marinade and let it simmer for 10 minutes. Then, add the white gravy and bring the tikka masala back to a boil.

2. Serve: Just before serving, add the heavy cream and chopped cilantro. Taste; add salt and chili powder to your liking. Serve paneer tikka masala over basmati rice.

~ D'AFRIC ~

FALAFEL

 MAKES
About 30 large falafel

Don't be scared by the prospect of deep-frying at home: as long as you're carefully not to let any water or other liquids come in contact with the hot oil, it should be a stress-free experience, with fantastically delicious falafel as your reward.

 TIME
Total Time: 1 hour
Active Time: 30 minutes

 INGREDIENTS
2 cups (480 grams) cooked chickpeas, drained
1 medium yellow onion, roughly chopped
1/4 cup (25 grams) roughly chopped fresh parsley
1/4 cup (25 grams) roughly chopped fresh cilantro
2 teaspoons salt
1 teaspoon red pepper flakes
6 cloves of garlic
2 teaspoons cumin
1/2 teaspoons baking powder
1 cup (130 grams) all-purpose or chickpea flour, plus more as needed
2-3 cups (480-720 mL) neutral oil, for frying

 PREPARATION

1. Make the falafel dough: Place the drained chickpeas and onion in the bowl of a food processor. Blend for 30 seconds, then add the parsley, cilantro, salt, hot pepper, garlic, and cumin. Process until well blended but not pureed. (If you don't have a food processor, you can also finely mash this mixture with a fork or potato masher.)

2. Sprinkle in the baking powder and 1/2 cup of the flour and pulse. Continue adding flour little by little until a slightly sticky dough forms. (It should be just dry enough that you can take a piece and roll it into a ball with your hands.)

3. Chill: Place the dough in a bowl, cover, and refrigerate for at least 30 minutes or up to 12 hours.

4. Fry: In a large, wide pan, add oil until you have a depth of about 1/2 inch. (For a pan 11 inches in diameter, you'll need about 3 cups of oil.) Heat the oil over high heat. Shape the chilled falafel dough into balls 1 1/2 - 2 inches in diameter. Carefully place the balls into the hot oil; they should sizzle slightly on contact. Fry until the bottom side is golden brown, about 4 minutes, then flip and cook another 3-4 minutes, until the falafel are golden brown and crispy all over. Use a slotted spoon to place them onto a paper towel-lined plate. Continue cooking in batches as needed.

5. Serve: Falafel are fantastic on their own or served with salata aswat (see page 32) or labneh (see page 14). Or, put together many different recipes to make a falafel wrap: simply combine hummus, labneh falafel, and chopped tomato in a tortilla or grilled flatbread (like Osteria's, page 156).

~ JUNIPER SOCIAL ~

ASIAN SLAW

SERVES
4

This is a fantastic go-to lunch recipe. The rice, tofu, and hearty dose of vegetables will keep you full, and the peanut sauce adds a beautiful punch of flavor.

TIME
Total Time: 45 minutes
Active Time: 45 minutes

INGREDIENTS FOR THE PEANUT SAUCE

2 teaspoons tamarind paste
1 1/2 tablespoons soy sauce
Juice of 1 large lime
1 small red chilli, finely chopped
1/2 teaspoon garlic, finely minced
1 teaspoon grated ginger
1 tablespoon honey
1/3 cup (85 grams) smooth, unsweetened peanut butter
1/3 - 1/2 cup (80 - 120 mL) hot water
1 tablespoon finely chopped cilantro

FOR THE MARINADE

3 tablespoons soy sauce
3 tablespoons honey

FOR THE SALAD

8 ounces (230 grams) firm tofu
2 zucchini, cut into thin rounds
3 carrots, peeled and ribboned with a vegetable peeler
1 1/2 (170 grams) cups grated red cabbage
2 cups (240 grams) cooked brown rice]

EXTRAS

1 tablespoon neutral oil, for the pan
Olive oil and a handful of chopped cilantro, to garnish

PREPARATION

1. Make the peanut sauce: Combine the tamarind paste, soy sauce, lime juice, chilli, garlic, ginger, and honey in a medium mixing bowl. Stir until well combined. Add the peanut butter and mix well. Slowly add hot water to thin the sauce, then set it aside.

2. Prepare the tofu: First, press the moisture out of the block of tofu by wrapping it in a double layer of paper towel and pressing down. Then, cut the tofu into slices about 1/2" wide. In a medium bowl, combine 3 tablespoons soy sauce and 3 tablespoons honey. Coat the tofu strips in the marinade and let them rest for at least 10 minutes.

3. Cook the tofu: Heat 1 tablespoon of oil in a large skillet. Strain the tofu out of the marinade, reserving the remaining marinade in a medium bowl. When the oil is very hot but not yet smoking, place the tofu strips in the pan. (Be careful, as the tofu may splatter a bit when it meets the oil; tongs are useful here.) Cook the tofu for about 2 minutes, until the bottom side is nicely browned, then flip and cook for another 90 seconds. Depending on the size of your pan, you may have to do this in two batches to avoid crowding the tofu.

4. Cook the zucchini: Toss the sliced zucchini in the remaining soy/honey marinade. Add another 1/2 tablespoon of oil to the pan, then add the zucchini. Resist the urge to stir them around: if you let them cook for 1-2 minutes undisturbed, they will brown beautifully. Once that time is up, give the zucchini a stir and cook them for 2 minutes more, until they are tender and nicely caramelized.

5. Construct: Layer the brown rice, ribboned carrots, grated cabbage, zucchini, and tofu in 4 individual bowls. Drizzle with the peanut sauce and a little olive oil. Garnish with a generous handful of chopped cilantro.

NOTES

Steps one and two can be done a day ahead of time.

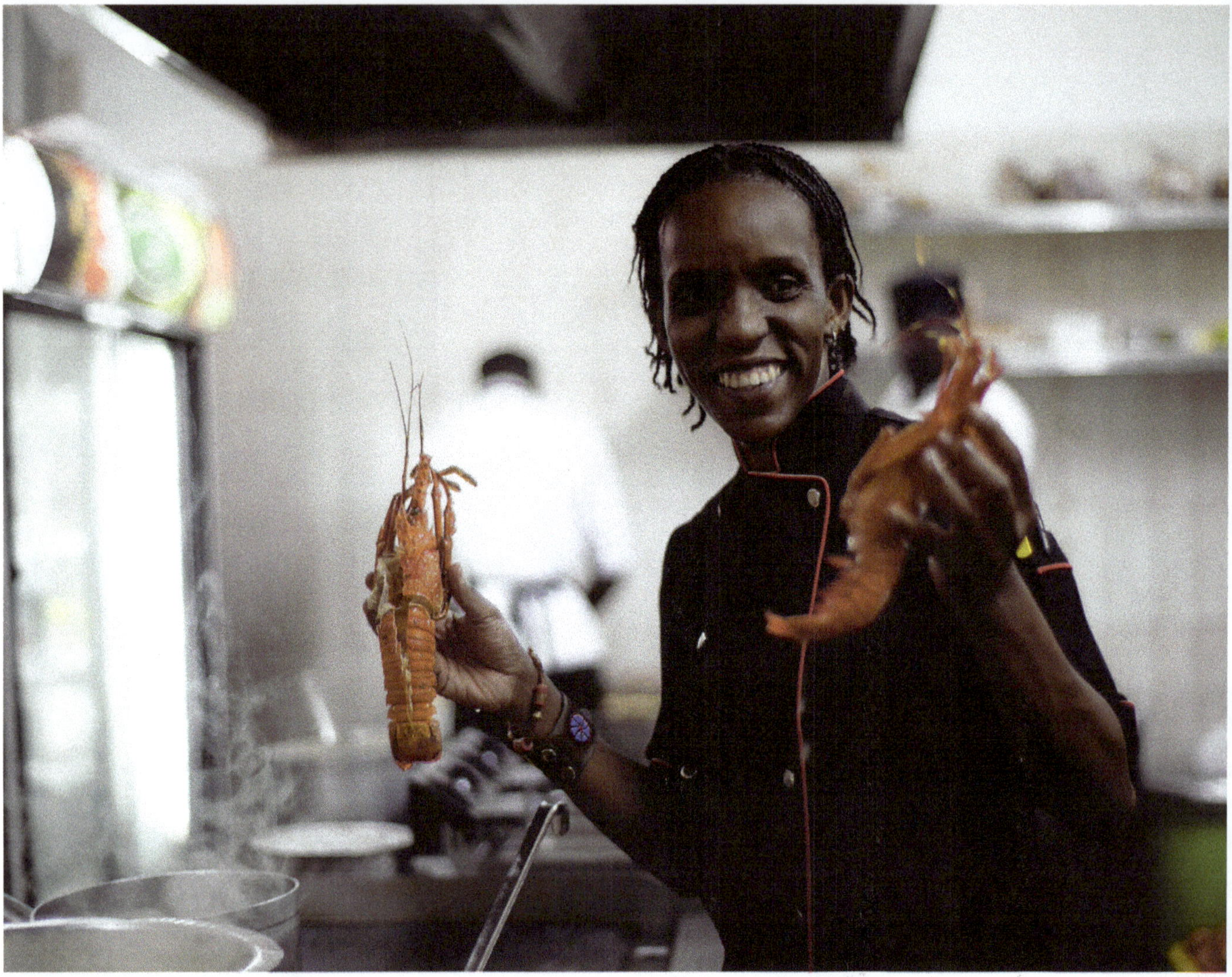

MONIKOS

Wine of the Month
FOOTPRINT
THE LONG WALK
FOOTPRINT
SOUTH AFRICA
Chenin blanc Semillion
@ 500/=
Chardonnay
Shiraz
@ 2250/=
Merlot
Cabernet Sauvignon
WINES OF ORIGIN WESTERN CAPE!

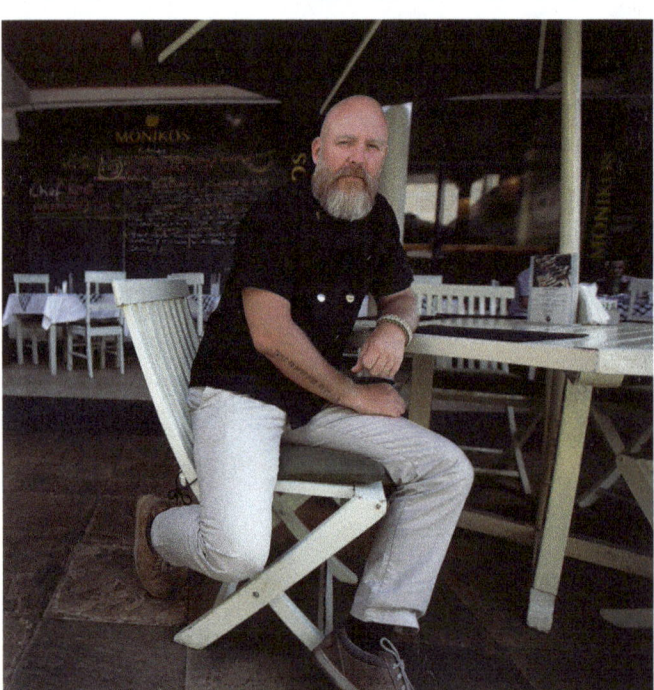

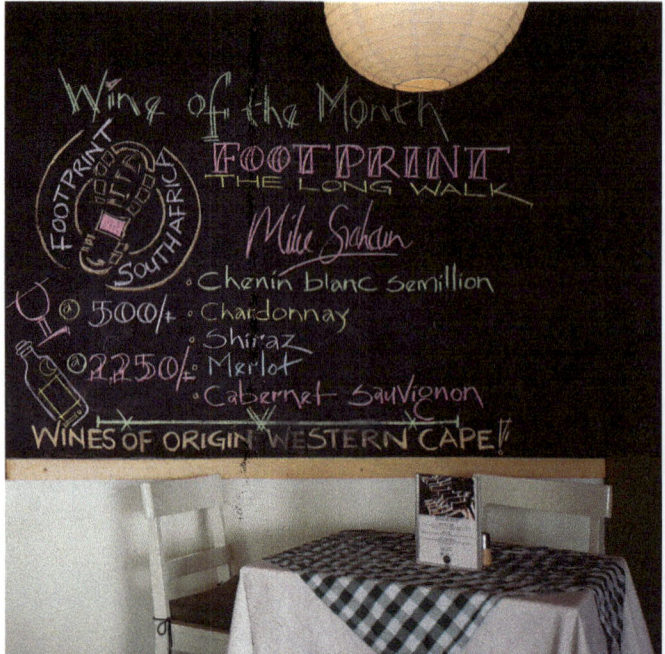

Moniko's

Claes and Jonas met in Nairobi, but act as if they've known each other forever. Both Swedes, they came to Nairobi for different reasons, but their shared love for food and drink brought them together to open Moniko's Kitchen.

Claes was what today we call a digital nomad. He worked in corporate IT for thirty-five years all around Europe before quitting his job and moving to Nairobi to give a go at a new life. It was here that he met Jonas, who in many ways is his opposite. Claes is buttoned up and very proper, soft spoken and understated. Jonas has a big personality, a big voice and a big, shiny bald head that seems to be perpetually sunburned.

Jonas arrived in Nairobi by fluke. While in university in Sweden, he saw a posting on a bulletin board for a job in a safari camp in the Masai Mara. On a whim, he applied and got the job. Immediately after he graduated, he hopped on a plane headed to Kenya. He worked in the camp for nine months and then spent the next twenty years working in the tourism industry.

In 2008, Claes and Jonas decided to open the restaurant in Nairobi. The post-election violence of the previous year had all but shut down the tourism industry, and both found themselves with time on their hands. They'd noticed a clear gap in the market for restaurants serving simple but good lunch foods, and decided that they would open a place that would be "homey, hearty and healthy." Moniko's Kitchen was born.

For the first four years, they only served lunch, but by 2012, the economy had started to recover and they decided to open for breakfast and dinner.

A unique aspect of Nairobi life is that for most of the city's middle and upper-class inhabitants, life revolves around shopping malls. People go to malls for restaurants, supermarkets, leisure time and shopping. However, in 2013 when the Westgate Shopping Mall shooting happened, people's shopping habits changed. Many people started avoiding malls, preferring smaller shopping centers. Moniko's is located in a small, neighborhood mall called Valley Arcade, and Claes noted that their business grew markedly after Westgate.

Today, Moniko's is a bustling restaurant, with fashionistas lunching next to politicians in the outdoor garden. While they're best known for salads and sandwiches, Jonas, an eager and passionate cook, has added some Scandinavian dishes to the menu that he likes to prepare at home. Jonas collects cookbooks and is obsessed with the Food Network's Diners, Drive-ins and Dives. He loves experimenting with cuisines and his influences are evident in the restaurant, where Thai curries share a page with poached salmon with dill.

In Masai, the work moniko means fearless. Jonas gave this name to his son, and he and Claes gave this name to their restaurant. Like their peers across the city who left their homes for a new life in Nairobi, whether they realize it or not, they're all fearless.

LA SALUMERIA

RAVIOLI WITH RICOTTA & SPINACH

 MAKES
about 30 large ravioli (or 40 smaller ones)

If you'd like to take a leaf out of La Salumeria's book and make homemade ricotta cheese, it's quite easy: simply bring 3 cups (720 mL) of whole milk to a boil, then turn off the heat and add 1/3 cup lemon juice. When the milkfat has separated from the whey, strain it through a fine-mesh strainer. When it's well strained, add a pinch of salt.

 TIME
Total Time: 1.5 hours
Active Time: 1 hour

 SPECIAL TOOLS
Circular cookie cutters or jars, 2"-3" in diameter; pastry brush

 INGREDIENTS FOR THE PASTA DOUGH
2 cups (260 grams) flour
Pinch of salt
4 - 5 eggs

FOR THE FILLING
1 teaspoon baking soda
8 ounces (230 grams) fresh or frozen spinach
1 egg
1 cup (225 grams) ricotta cheese
1/4 teaspoon ground nutmeg

TO CONSTRUCT
1 egg
1/2 teaspoon salt
A few grinds of black pepper

TO SERVE
2 tablespoons olive oil
1/2 cup (50 grams) parmesan cheese

 PREPARATION

1. Make the pasta dough: In a large bowl, combine the flour, salt, and 4 eggs and stir to combine. If the dough is a bit dry, add the fifth egg. Stir until a rough dough forms, then knead it on a clean surface until it is smooth and springy. Place the dough in a clean bowl, cover, and chill in the fridge for at least 30 minutes.

2. Prepare the filling: Boil a large pot of water and add the baking soda (which helps the spinach keep its color), then the spinach; boil the spinach for three minutes, then strain and rinse the spinach in cold water and squeeze out all the extra moisture. (If you're using frozen spinach, skip the boiling; just squeeze the moisture out of the spinach once it has thawed.) Roughly chop the cooled spinach and blend it with the egg, ricotta, nutmeg, salt, and pepper.

3. Roll the pasta: Divide the pasta dough into two balls. Roll each ball into a very thin sheet. Use a round cookie cutter or a jar to cut circles out of the dough, re-rolling the scraps as you go until all the dough has been cut into circles.

4. Fill the pasta: Lightly beat the egg in a small dish. Place a small dollop of filling in the middle of half the circles of dough. Brush the other half of the circles with egg. Place the egg-washed circles over the filling and use your fingers to press down gently around the filling to remove air bubbles. Then, use the tines of a fork to firmly press the edges of each ravioli closed.

5. Boil the pasta: Prepare a large pot of lightly salted boiling water. Carefully place the ravioli in the boiling water and stir gently to keep them from sticking to the bottom. The ravioli will float to the top after 2-3 minutes; continue to boil for two minutes more after they float, then strain them out with a slotted spoon.

6. Serve: Place a half-dozen ravioli in a pasta bowl. Drizzle with olive oil, sprinkle with parmesan cheese, and garnish with a few grinds of black pepper.

~ CHOWPATY ~

GARLIC BUTTER MASALA DOSA

 **SERVES**
6 large dosas

Making a perfect dosa takes some practice, so don't be discouraged if your first one isn't an instant success. A nonstick or well seasoned cast iron pan will be your best friend in dosa making. If you have the option of either one, go for the nonstick: its lighter weight will make swirling the dosa batter easier.

 TIME
Total Time: 1 hour
Active Time: 13-25 hours

INGREDIENTS FOR THE DOSA BATTER
2 1/4 cups (350 grams) rice flour
1 cup (115 grams) lentil or gram flour (also called besan)
1 2/3 cup (400 mL) water, divided
1 teaspoon sugar
1 teaspoon salt

FOR THE FILLING
6 large potatoes, peeled and cut into wedges
6 tablespoons (85 grams) butter or ghee, divided
2 heads garlic, peeled and very finely minced
2 small yellow onions, thinly sliced
1 tablespoon garam masala spice
1/2 teaspoon turmeric
1 teaspoon salt, plus more to taste
Handful of fresh chopped cilantro

 PREPARATION

1. **The day before, pre-ferment the batter:** Mix the rice flour and lentil flour with 1 1/3 cups (320 mL) water. Stir thoroughly. Cover with plastic wrap or a clean kitchen towel and let rest for 12 hours or up to 24 hours. The next day, add the sugar, salt, and additional 1/3 cup (80 mL) water and stir. The batter should be thin, similar to a crêpe batter; if it isn't, slowly add water to thin it.

2. **Cook the potatoes:** Place the potato wedges in a medium pot and cover them with cold, lightly salted water; bring the water to a boil and cook the potatoes until they are fork tender, about 20 minutes. Drain the potatoes, rinse them in cold water, and chop them into small pieces.

3. **Make the filling:** Heat 2 tablespoons of butter over medium heat and fry the garlic until it's brown, about 1 minute. Add the onions, garam masala, turmeric, and salt. Cook until the onions are translucent and the spices are very aromatic, about 3 minutes. Remove from the heat and add the chopped potatoes, stirring to coat them in the spices. Add the chopped cilantro and salt. Taste; add more salt to your liking.

4. **Cook the dosas:** First, melt 3 tablespoons of butter and set it aside. Heat the last tablespoon of butter over medium heat in a large, round saucepan; use a paper towel to remove excess butter, keeping it on hand to regrease the pan after each dosa. Use a 1/2 cup (120 mL) measure to pour batter into the hot pan and immediately swirl the pan to spread the batter evenly and thinly. Let the dosa cook until you see bubbles appear and the surface looks dry, about 30 seconds. Spoon potato filling over one half of the dosa, then drizzle a half tablespoon of melted butter over. Use a spatula to fold the empty half over the filling. Cook another 30 seconds, pressing down on the filling, before carefully transferring the dosa to a plate. Regrease the pan and continue with the remaining batter and filling.

Meat Mains

132	SOUTHERN BISCUIT SAMMY	Marula Mercantile
136	JERK CHICKEN	Taste of Jamaica
137	JERK SEASONING MIX	Taste of Jamaica
140	HOT POT	Little Sheep
142	SHUI ZHU PORK	Chengdu Impressions
146	MURG MAKHANI (BUTTER CHICKEN)	Open House
148	DUCK CONFIT & GRATIN POTATOES WITH MUSHROOM SAUCE	Belle Ambiance
150	PYTT-I-PANNA (PUT IN THE POT)	Moniko's
154	SCALLION DUMPLINGS	Afghan House
156	PIZZA DOUGH	Osteria
158	DIAVOLO PIZZA	Osteria
162	HUI GUO ROU (TWICE-COOKED PORK)	Chengdu Impressions
164	BEEF BURGER	Purdy Arms
166	CARAMELIZED ONIONS	Purdy Arms
170	MEAT PATTIES	Taste of Jamaica
172	CHICKEN TERIYAKI	Cheka
176	STEAK SKEWERS	Fogo Gaucho
180	PORK KATSUDON	Sushi Soo
182	PASTA CARBONARA	Trattoria
184	FEIJOADA	Fogo Gaucho
188	MUTTON SHORVA	Afghan House

MARULA MERCANTILE

SOUTHERN BISCUIT SAMMY

 SERVES
about 6

In a land where the Queen's English dictates that a biscuit is sweet, there is a nice nostalgia for Americans to see that Marula's biscuit is no such thing: it's a buttery, high rising quick bread that makes your kitchen instantly smell like heaven. Paired with a hand-mixed sausage patty and fried egg, this is ideal brunch food.

 TIME
Total Time: 45 minutes
Active Time: 45 minutes

 PREPARATION: FOR THE BISCUITS

1. Preheat the oven to 350 F (175C).

2. Make the dough: In a large bowl, combine the flour, sugar, baking powder, and salt. Cut the butter into pieces and add it to the flour mixture; use your fingers to break up the butter until it's in no more than pea-sized bits. Add the eggs and buttermilk and stir to combine. (The dough should be dry enough to knead without sticking to your hands; if it isn't, add up to a cup of flour.)

3. Cut the dough: Turn the dough onto a lightly floured surface. Knead gently to bring it together. Then, use a rolling pin to roll the dough to about 1/2 inch thick. Use a glass, biscuit cutter, or knife to cut the dough into rounds or squares about 3 inches across.

4. Bake: Place the biscuits on an ungreased baking sheet, leaving at least 1 inch between them. Bake for 10-12 minutes, until the biscuits are golden on top and bottom. Brush the tops with melted butter. Serve warm with butter & jam or with sausage & egg (see below).

INGREDIENTS: FOR THE BUTTERMILK BISCUIT

3 cups (390 grams) flour
2 tablespoons granulated sugar
2 tablespoons baking powder
1 teaspoon salt
1/2 cup (115 grams) very cold unsalted butter
2 eggs
3/4 cup (180 grams) buttermilk (or plain yogurt)
2 tablespoons melted butter, for brushing

FOR THE SAUSAGE PATTY

18 ounces (500 grams) pork mince
1/2 tablespoon ground black pepper
1/2 tablespoon brown sugar
1/2 teaspoon cayenne pepper
1/4 teaspoon ground nutmeg
1/2 tablespoon chopped sage
1/4 teaspoon chopped rosemary
1/2 tablespoon minced thyme
2 teaspoons salt
A little oil, for frying

FOR THE SAUSAGE PATTY

1. Make the patties: Combine the pork, black pepper, brown sugar, cayenne, nutmeg, herbs, and salt in a medium bowl. Use your hands to mix well. Portion into 6 patties (each one will weigh about 3 ounces/90 grams), taking care to make them about the same diameter as your biscuits.

2. Cook: Heat a little oil in a medium pan over medium-high heat. Fry the sausage patties until they are no longer pink in the middle, about 4 minutes per side. Set the patties aside while you prepare the eggs.

FOR THE EGGS

1. Fry the eggs: Heat a couple of tablespoons of oil or butter in a large pan over medium heat. Crack the eggs into the pan and let them cook until the edges begin to bubble and brown. Sprinkle with salt and pepper and cook, covered, for about 2 minutes. Place a slice of cheddar cheese on each egg and cover again just until the cheese is melted and the yolks are done to your liking.

2. Build your biscuit: Cut the warm biscuits in half. Place a sausage patty on the bottom half of the biscuit. Top it with a cheesy egg and the other half of the biscuit. Enjoy!

FOR THE SUNNY SIDE UP EGGS

6 eggs

6 cheddar cheese slices

Sprinkle of salt & pepper

Oil or butter, for frying

NOTES

If you want to have a lazy morning before brunch, you can make the biscuit dough and the pork patties the night before. Simply cover both with plastic wrap and keep them in the refrigerator overnight. If you are bothered by the idea of an egg that flops over the edge of your biscuit sandwich, you can use a circular metal cookie cutter as a mold when cracking your fried eggs into the pan.

Osteria

In the early 2000s, Maurizio Corti was dreaming of a new kind of Italian restaurant in Nairobi. He wanted it to be inspired by the Chianti region of Tuscany and make "sophisticated food, but served in a simpl way." When Maurizio Fregoni came to Nairobi in 2008 on holiday, he met Corti and the two hit it off. Fregoni left his job in Spain and now, seven years later, Fregoni and Corti are co-managing La Osteria, which has grown to have multiple branches and a gelato stand.

There is no wifi at the restaurant; both Maurizios hold firm to the idea that if you come to eat, you come to eat. The restaurant features over 70 different wines including many so-called "super Tuscan" wines. They estimate that 90% of the food consumed in the restaurant is produced not just in Kenya but by Osteria staff, either at their sprawling compound in the Kilimani neighborhood or at the farm they maintain in Naivasha. They buy the milk for their house-made ricotta and mozzarella from small herds of cows grazed on the slopes of Mount Kenya, a verdant region that produces milk with the high butterfat content they need.

Many of the staff at La Osteria are originally from the Kenyan coast. There is a well-established Italian presence on the south coast, and the area is well endowed with hyper-authentic Italian restaurants serving up freshly-caught fish and seafood. As a result, there are many Kenyan chefs well trained in Italian cooking (and the Italian language: tourists on the beach are often regaled first in Italian, then Kiswahili, then English). Election-related and inter-tribal violence caused a major slump in tourism in 2007, just around the time that the Maurizios were setting up shop. They offered employment in Nairobi to a handful of recently jobless chefs, many of whom have been with the restaurant ever since.

Jefwa, one of their most seasoned employees, missed the opportunity to attend secondary school because his family was unable to pay the school fees. Then, he was injured in a road accident that left him minus one thumb. Now a manager at La Osteria, he frequents the pizza station, where patrons watch him twirling pizza dough high in the air with ease.

As we watched Jefwa throw pizza after pizza into La Osteria's huge oven, Maurizio Fregoni came back to the vision that he and Maurizio Corti started with. "Our menu is 99% Italian, I think," he said. "But we do have Paella Tuesday. After 18 years in Spain, I had to bring the paella with me!"

~ TASTE OF JAMAICA ~

JERK CHICKEN

 SERVES
3-4

There are infinite variations on jerk chicken, and anyone who has one is bound to insist theirs is the best. We have no problem promising that Taste of Jamaica's is the best we've had. The quantity of barbecue sauce listed here will be much more than you'll need, which is good since you'll definitely want to make this chicken again very soon.

 TIME
Total Time: 1 hour 15 minutes (or up to 9 hours)
Active Time: 45 minutes

 INGREDIENTS
about 1 1/2 pound (680 grams) chicken breasts and/or legs

FOR THE MARINADE
6 garlic cloves, peeled and smashed
6 scallions, white & green parts, roughly chopped
1 Scotch bonnet or jalapeño pepper (or 1/2 of one, for a less spicy result), minced
1 thumb-sized piece of fresh ginger, peeled and roughly chopped
2 tablespoons white vinegar
2 tablespoons water
1 tablespoon brown sugar
2 tablespoons jerk spice mix (see page 137)

FOR THE BARBECUE SAUCE
1 1/4 cups (280 grams) ketchup
1 teaspoon honey (optional)
1 teaspoon tamarind paste
1 teaspoon Worcestershire sauce
1 teaspoon dijon mustard
1 teaspoon red wine vinegar
1 tablespoon jerk spice mix
1/2 teaspoon salt

PREPARATION
1. First, prepare the marinade: Place all the marinade ingredients in the bowl of a food processor. Blend until you have a smooth paste.

2. Marinate the chicken: Use a sharp paring knife to make shallow cuts all over your chicken. Rub the marinade all over the chicken. Let the chicken rest for at least 30 minutes or for up to 8 hours in the fridge.

3. Preheat the oven to 350F (175 C) or heat a grill to medium - high.

4. Roast: Roast or grill the chicken for about 25 minutes. Then, make a small cut into the center of the largest piece of meat; if you see pink, continue cooking and checking in 5 minute increments. Or, use a thermometer to check that the internal temperature reaches 165F (74C).

5. While the chicken is cooking, **make the barbecue sauce:** Combine all the sauce ingredients in a small saucepan. Bring to a low simmer and cook, stirring, for 5 - 8 minutes, until the mixture has thickened very slightly. Take off the heat and let it cool to room temperature. Taste and adjust the seasoning to your liking.

6. Finish: Remove the chicken from the oven and increase the temperature to 400C (200C). Slather the chicken with barbecue sauce, place it on a baking sheet, and broil to 2-3 minutes, until sauce on the chicken begins to caramelize.

7. Serve: Serve jerk chicken fresh out of the oven with a generous side of rice and peas (see page 96).

~~~ TASTE OF JAMAICA ~~~

JERK SEASONING SPICE MIX

YIELD
1/4 cup

Make a big batch of this and keep it in your spice cabinet for easy prep.

TIME
Total Time: 5 minutes
Active Time: 5 minutes

PREPARATION

1. Combine all the ingredients in a small jar with a lid. Stir or shake well to combine.

INGREDIENTS
1 teaspoon cayenne pepper
2 teaspoons dried thyme
2 teaspoons dried oregano
1 teaspoon paprika
1 teaspoon nutmeg
1/2 teaspoon red pepper flakes
1/2 teaspoon ground black pepper
1/4 teaspoon cinnamon
2 teaspoons sugar
2 teaspoons salt
2 teaspoons garlic powder, optional

Abyssinia

Many of the restaurateurs in this book arrived at their profession somewhat accidentally, but Abebe has always had a passion for hospitality. Born in Ethiopia, he moved to Kenya over thirty years ago. He spent six and a half years studying hotel management in Nairobi and moved into the exporting business after graduation, collecting and selling antiques and artifacts. During that time, he got married and had three children. Six years ago, he decided to return to his roots in hospitality and open a restaurant. Abyssinia grew out of a pride for his own culture and cuisine, and a desire to share it with others.

Talking with Abebe about food is like reading an encyclopedia about Ethiopian cuisine. He talks passionately about cooking and spices, reminiscing about the way his mother used to make kitfo, his favorite food and the main dish of his tribe. Kitfo, for the uninitiated, is minced raw beef, similar to tartare, marinated in spices and clarified butter. It's one of the most popular dishes served at the restaurant, and it's made even more special by the fact that Abebe's wife makes the clarified butter at home according to a secret recipe.

The restaurant itself is a bungalow that's been converted, with various dining spaces and awnings that stretch into a garden. Trees seem to grow through the floor in places, and you feel like you're simultaneously sitting in a forest and in a cozy living room. Off to the side of the dining area a woman sits on a low stool surrounded by tiny coffee cups. She prepares traditional Ethiopian coffee to order, roasting the coffee beans and making fresh popcorn. The smell of the coffee and popping corn waft through the air, entreating you to hurry and finish your meal so you can get onto the next course. v

When asked if Nairobi feels like home, Abebe responded that in his thirty years here, he has never felt like an outsider. He is a Kenyan citizen and Nairobi is his home.

~ LITTLE SHEEP ~

HOT POT

 SERVES
6 - 8

In an ideal world, you would have a dedicated hot pot pot, which has a divider in the middle that allows you to have a mild broth and a spicy broth simmering over a single burner. If you don't have such a pot, you'll have to either set up two burners or decide which style of broth appeals to your party and serve that one alone. If you're only serving the spicy broth, double the quantity given below. Hot pot can very easily be vegetarian, of course: simply up the quantities of vegetables, noodles, and tofu and omit the meat.

 TIME
Total Time: 1.5 hours
Active Time: 30 minutes

 SPECIAL TOOLS
Special equipment: freestanding burner(s), divided pot (or a single large pot or wok), chopsticks (2 pairs per person), two slotted spoons, ladle

 INGREDIENTS FOR THE MILD BROTH
2 pounds (900 grams) chicken meat, 10-12 chicken bones, or a whole chicken carcass
2 large carrots, roughly chopped
2 celery stalks, roughly chopped
4 green onions, chopped
1 large piece of ginger, sliced
8 cloves of garlic, peeled and smashed
6 whole black peppercorns
16-18 cups (4-4 ½ litres) water
1 tablespoon salt, plus more to taste

 PREPARATION: FOR THE BROTHS

1. Make the mild broth: Place all the broth ingredients in a large pot. Bring the liquid to a boil, then reduce the heat and simmer for about one hour, skimming impurities that rise to the surface every 20 minutes. Pass the liquid through a fine mesh strainer and set it aside.

2. Make the spicy broth: In a large pot or wok, heat the oil over medium-high heat. Add the ginger, garlic, peppercorns, chili pepper, star anise, cinnamon, and fennel and stir until the garlic starts to brown and the spices are very aromatic, about 3 minutes. Add the sugar and stir to coat the spices. Slowly pour in the water. Simmer the broth for 30 minutes. At this point, you can either strain the spices out from the broth or leave them in. (Little Sheep leaves the spices in their broth.)

FOR THE SAUCES

1. Make the peanut sauce: In a small bowl, stir together the peanut butter, soy sauce, bean paste, and sugar. Slowly whisk in the hot water until the sauce is thinned to your liking. Add salt to taste.

2. Make the sesame sauce: In another bowl, stir together the tahini, Hoisin sauce, chili paste, and sesame oil. Add salt to taste.

TO SERVE

1. Prepare the table: Set up your burner(s) in the middle of a large table and bring the stock(s) to a rolling boil. Put the sauces and add-ins in bowls and set them around the table. Give each person two pairs of chopsticks and a personal bowl.

2. Cook & Eat: Put your add-ins of choice into the broth(s), taking care not to add so much at one time that the broth stops boiling. Use a slotted spoon or chopsticks to fish things out of the broth once they're cooked, then ladle broth into your personal bowl. You can add sauces directly into your broth or keep them alongside to dip. If the level of liquid in the communal pot gets low, add more water or broth and let it come back to a boil before continuing.

FOR THE SPICY BROTH

2 tablespoons neutral oil

1 tablespoon fresh ginger, peeled and sliced

1 whole head of garlic, cloves peeled and smashed

1 teaspoon Sichuan peppercorns

1 tablespoon dried chili pepper, chopped

2 star anise pods (optional)

3 cinnamon sticks

½ teaspoon fennel seeds

2 teaspoons sugar

8 cups mild broth

FOR THE PEANUT DIPPING SAUCE

½ cup (125 grams) smooth peanut butter

1 tablespoon soy sauce

1 tablespoon chili bean paste

2 teaspoons sugar

¼ cup (60 mL) hot water, plus more as needed

Pinch of salt (if your peanut butter is unsalted)

FOR THE SESAME DIPPING SAUCE

½ cup (70 grams) tahini paste

1 teaspoon Hoisin sauce

1 teaspoon chili paste

2 tablespoons sesame oil

Salt, to taste

SUGGESTED ADD-INS

1-2 pounds (450-900 grams) paper-thin beef ribeye or lamb (ask your butcher to slice it)

7 ounces (200 grams) needle mushrooms, Chinese black mushrooms, or shiitake mushrooms

10 ounces (285 grams) tofu skins

2 large blocks extra-firm tofu, cut into cubes

12 ounces (340 grams) fresh udon noodles or dried vermicelli

Fresh or frozen dumplings

4 bunches baby bok choy, leaves separated from the root

1 large daikon radish, thinly sliced

2 lotus roots, thinly sliced

2 large handfuls mung bean sprouts

NOTES

Why two pairs of chopsticks per person? Etiquette dictates that diners use one pair of chopsticks in the communal broth and a separate pair for eating. This also helps prevent foodborne illness from raw meat. If your hot pot is vegetarian and you're comfortable with everyone at your table, one pair per person is fine.

~ CHENGDU IMPRESSIONS ~

SHUI ZHU PORK

 SERVES
2-3

This delicious preparation of pork comes together surprisingly quickly. If you can't find mung bean sprouts, you can also use soybean sprouts.

 TIME
Total Time: 20 minutes
Active Time: 20 minutes

 INGREDIENTS

1-2 cups (170 - 340 grams) steamed white rice
10 ounces (280 grams) lean pork, cut into thin strips
½ teaspoon ground white pepper
2 teaspoons cornstarch, divided
Pinch of salt
2 tablespoons + ½ cup (150 mL) oil, divided
8 ounces (225 grams) mung bean sprouts
¼ head Napa cabbage (about 8 ounces / 225 grams), finely chopped
1 teaspoon chili bean paste (dou ban jiang)
1 teaspoon minced ginger
1 teaspoon minced garlic
½ teaspoon + a pinch Sichuan peppercorn powder
1 ½ cups (360 mL) chicken stock
1 teaspoon soy sauce
½ teaspoon sugar
Handful chopped green garlic (or green onions)

 PREPARATION

1. Prep your serving bowls: Divide the rice among two or three serving bowls.

2. Prepare the pork: Place the pork in a small bowl. Sprinkle it with the white pepper, 1 teaspoon cornstarch, and a pinch of salt and toss to coat.

3. Cook the vegetables: Heat 1 tablespoon of oil in a wok over high heat. Add the sprouts and cabbage and a pinch of salt and cook, stirring, until the cabbage just starts to brown, about 5 minutes. Remove the veggies from the wok and place them in the serving bowls, atop the rice.

4. Make the sauce: Return the wok to the heat and add 1 tablespoon of oil. Once it's hot, add the chili bean paste, ginger, garlic, and ½ teaspoon Sichuan peppercorn powder and cook for 1-2 minutes. Add the stock, soy sauce and sugar and bring the liquid back to a boil.

5. Cook the pork: Add the pork to the wok and cook for 5-7 minutes, until the pork is cooked through. Add 1 teaspoon cornstarch and stir to incorporate. Let the sauce simmer for 2-3 minutes, until it has thickened slightly.

6. Construct: Place slices of pork on top of each bowl, then drizzle extra sauce over. Garnish with green garlic and a pinch of Sichuan peppercorn powder.

7. Finish: Heat ½ cup (120 mL) oil in a small pot until it's very hot, about 2 minutes, and carefully spoon it over the bowls of vegetables and pork.

8. Serve: Serve with a little extra soy sauce, as needed.

Belle Ambiance

"I had a choice between Nairobi and Paris. So I chose Nairobi."

So begins Laurent Schneider's tale of the winding road that brought him to Kenya. He began working at the tender age of 14, eventually making his way into the kitchens of several Michelin-starred restaurants in and around Paris. When the opportunity to take a high-level position in Kuwait came along, he took it. You can't buy wine in Kuwait, so Laurent found himself taking a stab at turning grape juice into wine in the back of his own pantry using a system of hermetic sealing he rigged up himself. "Suddenly, one day, I hear this huge explosion," he merrily recounted. He thought there were attacks in the street—this was 1990, after all—but, it turns out, "it was just all my wine bottles exploding. Trapped pressure, you know."

After long stints at some of the most prestigious hotels in East Africa, including Nairobi's InterContinental and Addis Ababa's Sheraton, Laurent found himself hankering for something more unique. "You go to a hotel in Timbuktu, New York, Phuket, they're all basically the same," he lamented. He wanted a restaurant that truly reflected its location and heritage, somewhere he could fuse French boudin noir with traditional Maasai technique to make a goat-blood black pudding. He wanted to make jars of tree tomato jam and passion fruit curd, using local ingredients instead of imported luxury goods. And so, in 2010, Belle Ambiance was born.

On our first visit, Belle Ambiance had just moved from its original location (which Cheka would later take over) to a new spot, closer to the Karen neighborhood, and the scene was cheerfully hectic. The restaurant, not yet open to diners, was filled with chefs doing everything from testing the coffee machine to stringing up fairy lights in the spacious garden. Laurent sipped a wine and mused about French arrogance in all things wine—"there are really quite a few good South African and Chilean wine suppliers here, and you get much better value for the quality"—but admitted that there's one thing he does deeply miss about Paris, a place he hasn't returned to for almost three years: the constant opportunity to go to professional operas, new art exhibits, museum installations, classical concerts, and plays.

"Yeah, we take our kids to online exhibitions," he says, "but there's no proof there that people beyond your parents like this stuff. That's what I miss."

Ã

NOTE
Belle Ambiance closed in early 2016.

—◇— OPEN HOUSE —◇—

MURG MAKHANI (BUTTER CHICKEN)

 **SERVES**
6

It's pretty much impossible to order anything disappointing at Open House, but this butter chicken curry goes above and beyond. There, this pale orange-colored curry comes to the table in a small pot and is set on a rack over a lit candle.

 TIME
Total Time: 45 minutes - 1 hour
Active Time: 45 minutes - 1 hour

 INGREDIENTS FOR THE CHICKEN

4 chicken breasts (about 18 ounces / 500 grams in total), cut into bite-size pieces
1 1/2 cups (340 grams) full-fat, plain yogurt
1 teaspoon cumin powder
1 teaspoon coriander powder
1 teaspoon lemon juice
1 teaspoon salt
1 tablespoon neutral oil

FOR THE TOMATO GRAVY

1 tablespoon butter or ghee
1 tablespoon oil
1 tablespoon minced garlic
1 tablespoon grated ginger
2 red onions, chopped
12 medium tomatoes, roughly chopped
1 teaspoon salt, plus more to taste
2 teaspoons chili powder, plus more to taste
1 cup (240 mL) water
2 tablespoons whole cashew nuts
1 cup (250 mL) heavy cream

TO SERVE

Cooked white rice
Handful of chopped cilantro

 PREPARATION

1. Marinate the chicken: In a large bowl, mix together the yogurt, cumin, coriander, lemon juice, and salt. Add the chicken and let it marinate for 30 minutes, or for up to 4 hours in the fridge.

2. Make the tomato gravy: In a large pot, heat the butter and oil. Add the garlic and ginger and cook, stirring, until they're very aromatic, about 3 minutes. Add the onions and cook until they are lightly browned, about 3 minutes more. Add the tomatoes, salt, and chili powder and cook for 15 minutes, pressing them occasionally with the back of a spoon to break them up. Add the water and the cashew nuts and let the sauce simmer for 5-7 minutes. Take it off the heat to cool slightly.

3. Blend the gravy: When the gravy is cool, thoroughly blend it in a food processor or blender.

4. Poach the chicken: Return the tomato gravy to the pot and bring it to a simmer over medium heat. Use a slotted spoon to remove the chicken from its marinade and add it to the tomato gravy; discard the leftover marinade. Simmer the chicken in the gravy for about 10 minutes. (If you are in doubt about the chicken's doneness, remove a piece and cut it in half; it should no longer be at all pink in the middle.)

5. Serve: Add the heavy cream and salt and stir to combine. Taste and add salt and chili powder as desired. Serve the curry over rice with fresh cilantro.

～ BELLE AMBIANCE ～

DUCK CONFIT & GRATIN POTATOES WITH MUSHROOM SAUCE

 **SERVES**
2

This dish is, for lack of a better adjective, very French. That is, it is quite rich, not skimping on butter or cream, with no acidic counterpoint in the recipe. The key to balance in this kind of dish is a good glass of wine. Try an acidic red, like a Beaujolais or Burgundy, for a perfect pairing.

 TIME
Total Time: 14 hours
Active Time: 1.5 hours

 INGREDIENTS: FOR THE DUCK
2 duck legs, fat left on
4 sprigs fresh rosemary, leaves removed and finely chopped
3 tablespoons salt
2 teaspoons black pepper
about 4 cups (1 litre) corn oil or duck fat
Sprinkle of fresh oregano, to garnish

FOR THE POTATOES
2 1/4 pounds (1 kg) potatoes, peeled and grated
1/2 cup (115 grams) unsalted butter
1/2 tablespoon salt
Pinch of nutmeg

FOR THE MUSHROOM SAUCE
4 tablespoons butter, divided
1 medium yellow onion, roughly chopped
1 cup (240 ml) dry white wine
1 cup (260 ml) heavy cream
2 cups (about 150 grams) fresh button mushrooms, cleaned and sliced
1/2 teaspoon salt

 PREPARATION: FOR THE DUCK

1. The night before: Mix the chopped rosemary, salt, and pepper together in a small bowl. Rub the mix all over the duck. Place the duck in a sealed container and let it rest in the fridge overnight.

2. Two hours before serving:
Preheat the oven to 355F (180C). Remove the duck from the fridge and rinse off the herb rub. Pat the legs dry with a paper towel or clean kitchen towel. Place the legs, skin side up, in a small baking dish and cover them completely with the corn oil or duck fat. Cover the dish with tin foil.

3. Bake: Place the duck in the preheated oven and let it cook for 2 hours, checking occasionally to ensure that the oil doesn't come to a boil (if it does, reduce the heat).

4. After 2 hours, remove the dish from the oven. Use tongs to remove the legs from the fat; place them on a paper towel-lined plate and let them cool.

5. Just before serving:
Turn your broiler on high. Place the legs on a baking sheet close to the top of the oven, skin side up, and broil for 2-3 minutes, just until the top side is nicely crisp.

FOR THE POTATOES

1. Dry the potatoes: Place a clean kitchen towel in a strainer. Place the grated potatoes in the towel, gather up the corners, and squeeze out as much moisture as you can. (The drier the potatoes, the better they will cook.)

2. Cook the potatoes: Heat the butter in a large skillet over medium-high heat. Add the potatoes, crowding them as little as possible, and sprinkle the salt and nutmeg over. Allow the potatoes to cook for five minutes before you touch them; they should begin to brown on the bottom side. Flip the potatoes, breaking up any clumps, and allow them to cook undisturbed for another five minutes. Continue cooking until they are golden all over, about 20 minutes in total.

FOR THE MUSHROOM SAUCE

1. Make the sauce: Melt 2 tablespoons butter in a wide skillet. Add the onion and cook for 2-3 minutes, until the onion is translucent. Add the white wine and cook until the wine has evaporated, 7-8 minutes. Add the cream and the mushrooms and cook for 5 more minutes, until the sauce begins to thicken.

2. Blend: Allow the sauce to cool for a couple of minutes before puréeing it in a blender until smooth. For a perfectly smooth sauce, pour it through a fine-mesh strainer, pressing it through with the back of a spoon or a spatula.

3. Monter au beurre: Return the sauce to the pan over low heat. Whisk in the final 2 tablespoons of butter. When the butter is melted, turn off the heat.

PUT IT ALL TOGETHER

1. Plate: To do as Ambiance does, press about 1 cup of cooked potatoes into a ramekin or round cup measure, packing them down thoroughly. Turn the mold over into the middle of a plate. The potatoes should make a nice geometrical mound on which to set the duck.

2. Garnish:
Drizzle the duck and potatoes with mushroom sauce and garnish with a sprig of fresh oregano and a few grinds of black pepper.

NOTES

Don't be too alarmed by the amount of fat used in this recipe. Although duck confit is *cooked* in somewhat alarming quantities of fat, it by no means absorbs all of that fat. In fact, post-cooking, nearly 3 3/4 cups of the 4 cups of fat used to cook the duck remain (and can be easily reused, if you strain the cooked oil through a paper towel-lined strainer and funnel it into a jar or bottle).

Monikos

PYTT-I-PANNA (PUT IN THE POT)

SERVES
4

This is classic Swedish leftover food: a comforting hash that you can throw all sorts of miscellaneous ingredients into. Moniko's reports that most customers ask for their egg to be fried; the traditional Swedish way, however, is to serve it raw, in its shell, atop the warm Pytt-i-Panna.

TIME
Total Time: 45 minutes
Active Time: 45 minutes

INGREDIENTS

2 large beetroots, peeled and cut into very small cubes

1 large onion, finely chopped

6 medium potatoes, cleaned and cut into very small cubes

1 chicken breast (7 ounces / 200 grams), cut into small cubes

7 ounces (200 grams) beef filet, cut into small cubes

2 gherkins, thinly sliced

4 eggs

6 tablespoons neutral oil, divided

Salt and pepper

Mustard (optional)

PREPARATION

1. Cook the beets: Preheat the oven to 400F (200C). Place the cubed beets on a tin foil-lined baking sheet. Sprinkle with 2 tablespoons of oil and a pinch of salt and roast until they're fork-tender, 15-20 minutes.

2. Prep the potatoes & meats: Meanwhile, place two skillets on the stove. Heat 2 tablespoons of oil in each of them. In one, cook the onions for 2-3 minutes; then, add the potatoes and cook, stirring, until they're golden on all sides and tender, about 15 minutes. In the other, fry the cubed chicken and beef filet together until they're browned and the chicken is cooked through, 8-10 minutes. Sprinkle salt generously over both skillets.

3. Construct: When the vegetables and meats are all cooked, stir them together in a medium bowl. Add the gherkins. Taste and add salt as needed.

4. Fry the eggs: Heat a tablespoon of butter or oil in a small pan. Fry the eggs, uncovered, for 2-3 minutes, then cover and cook until the yolks are done to your liking.

5. Serve: If you'd like to serve your pytt-i-panna with some extra flair, press the hash into a large measuring cup or a round mold and then turn it onto a plate. Top with the egg, a sprinkle of black pepper, and a generous dollop of mustard on the side.

NOTES

To make this dish vegetarian, simply replace the beef and chicken with vegetables of your choice. 2-3 zucchini and 1/2 a medium butternut squash stand in perfectly for the meat. Simply cut them into cubes of the same size as the beets and roast them, with a little oil and salt, until they're tender, 15-20 minutes.

Mama Ashanti

The first Mama Ashanti restaurant opened in Uganda in 2003 as a tiny fourteen seat Ghanaian eatery. But the original Mama Ashanti is Nana's mother, who developed all of the recipes in the restaurant and whose handwritten recipes he shared with us for this book. Nana describes the food that he serves in his Nairobi restaurant, opened in 2012, as "weekend home food." The type of food that you share with your family on the weekends when you're hanging out and enjoying each other's company.

Born and raised in northern Ghana, Nana moved to the UK at the age of twenty-one as a refugee. He worked as a sales representative for Honda for over twenty years, but always longed to return to Africa. In London, he met his wife, who is Ugandan, and decided to move with her to Uganda.

Cooking is in his blood, his mother ran a vocational cooking school in Ghana and his cousin was a chef, and throughout his time in the UK, he dreamt of someday opening a West African restaurant. They lived in a town called Bombo, near the capital of Kampala, and disappointed that he couldn't find any West African food, decided to open a restaurant himself.

Today, Mama Ashanti is a bustling restaurant with a lounge on one side that fills up in the evening, a garden that is frequented by families on the weekends, and an open grill and kitchen that sends the mouth-watering smells of fried plantains and grilled kebabs all over the premises. The majority of his customers are Kenyan, though he estimates that a quarter of his customers are West African. While many of the dishes are Ghanaian, the menu also includes Nigerian and Senegalese favorites like jollof rice and agusi with fish. Everything is made to order, which means that you might wait awhile for your order, but that means that you'll have time to munch on kelewe, fried plantains covered in spicy deliciousness, a classic street food in Ghana.

For Nana, running a Ghanaian restaurant is his passion – it's a food and culture that he loves, and that he wants to share. Many of his first-time customers have never had West African food before, and he's proud that he gets the opportunity to introduce them to his cuisine.

His dream is to grow the business into an East African chain someday, so that even more people can taste and fall in love with his mother's home cooking.

SCALLION DUMPLINGS

SERVES
4

These unique dumplings, paired with a rich meat sauce and finished with yogurt, are a beautiful and filling meal. To make a vegetarian version, simply replace the ground beef with an equivalent quantity of fresh tomatoes.

TIME
Total Time: 35 minutes
Active Time: 35 minutes

INGREDIENTS FOR THE SAUCE

5 tablespoons (70 grams) butter
1 shallot, minced
2 yellow onions, finely chopped
3 cloves garlic, minced
18 ounces (510 grams) ground beef
5 tablespoons tomato paste
2 ½ teaspoons coriander powder
1 tablespoon minced ginger
1 teaspoon salt, plus more to taste
1 cup (240 mL) water, plus more as needed
1 bay leaf

FOR THE DUMPLINGS

1 large leek, finely chopped
12 green onions, finely chopped, plus more for garnish
3 cloves garlic, minced
1 teaspoon red pepper flakes
1 teaspoon salt
1 egg
¼ cup (60 mL) water
48-60 round wrappers (storebought or homemade; see page XX)
Salt and pepper
2 cups (450 grams) yogurt, to garnish
Freshly ground black pepper

PREPARATION

1. Make the meat sauce: In a medium saucepan, melt the butter. Add the shallot, onions, and garlic. Cook, stirring, for 3-4 minutes, until the onions begin to lightly brown. Add the ground beef and stir until is has browned, 4-5 minutes. Add the tomato paste, coriander, ginger, and salt and stir to combine, then add 1 cup water and the bay leaf and let the mixture come to a boil. Reduce the heat to low and simmer the sauce while you make the dumplings. If the sauce starts to dry out while you make the dumplings, add water in ½ cup (120 mL) increments.

2. Make the dumpling filling: Combine the chopped leek, green onions, garlic, red pepper flakes, and salt in a medium bowl. Toss to combine.

3. Make the dumplings: Put a large pot of lightly salted water on to boil. In a small bowl, whisk together the egg and ¼ cup water. Place 2 dumpling wrappers on a clean work surface. Place 2 teaspoons of filling in the center of one of the wrappers; brush the other with the egg mixture and place it over the filling, pressing down to push out air bubbles, and firmly pinch the edges closed with your fingers. Continue making dumplings until you've used all the filling.

4. Boil the dumplings: Carefully drop the dumplings in the boiling water, then immediately place a lid on the pot. Boil for 3-4 minutes, then use a slotted spoon to strain out the dumplings. Set them aside.

5. Serve: Ladle a little of the sauce into the bottom of four shallow bowls. Place 6-7 dumplings in each bowl, then spoon more sauce over. Pour ½ cup of yogurt over each bowl. Garnish with chopped green onions and black pepper.

NOTES

If you're making the wonton wrappers yourself, you can make the process easier by rolling the dough out on a large, generously floured work surface and then using a jar to cut out circles. This will go faster than rolling out individual balls of dough.

~~~ OSTERIA ~~~

PIZZA DOUGH

MAKES
2 14-inch pizzas, or 4-6 6-inch ones

Some traditionalists cry foul at the notion of an egg in pizza dough—probably because they've never tried La Osteria's recipe, which is allowed to rise slowly in the fridge overnight and then rolled super-thin before getting 5 minutes in their woodburning oven.

TIME
Total Time: 2-14 hours
Active Time: 45 minutes

INGREDIENTS
1 cup (240 mL) warm (105F / 40C) water
1 1/2 teaspoons (5 grams) instant yeast
1 egg
1/4 cup (60 mL) olive oil
About 4 cups (520 grams) flour, plus more for rolling
1 tablespoon salt

PREPARATION

1. Test the yeast: Whisk together the warm water and the yeast in a medium bowl. Give the yeast 5 minutes to proof: you should see the bubbles beginning to form.

2. Make the dough: Add the egg and olive oil and stir to combine. Add 3 cups of the flour and the salt. Use a spatula to mix the flour gently into the yeast mixture. Gradually add the remaining flour until the dough is dry enough to be kneaded by hand.

3. Turn the dough out onto a lightly floured surface and knead for five minutes, adding flour if it's sticking, until the dough is stretchy and the surface is smooth and shiny.

4. Rise the dough: Let the dough rest for 10 minutes. Then, divide it into as many pieces as you'd like pizzas. Form each piece into a ball by tucking the ends under and pinching them together in the palms of your hands. To do as Osteria does, place the balls onto a small baking tray or dinner plates, sprinkle with flour, cover with a damp cloth or a sheet of plastic wrap, and let them rise in the fridge for 12 hours. For an expedited version, let the dough rise at room temperature for one or two hours.

5. Prebake: If your dough rose in the fridge, remove it from the fridge at least one hour before you want to bake. Once it has come to room temperature, use a rolling pin to roll the dough into circles of the desired size. Preheat the oven to 425F (220C) and place your rolled-out dough onto lightly greased baking sheets. Pre-bake each round for about 5 minutes, until they are barely golden on the top and bottom.

6. Make your pizzas: Top each round with your toppings of choice (see following page). Put the pizzas back into the hot oven to bake until the edges are browned and the toppings are warmed, about 8-10 minutes.

NOTES

1. Osteria serves every diner a beautiful, simple appetizer of a small flatbread. To do as they do, first brush a pre-baked dough generously with olive oil and sprinkle with salt and minced garlic. Bake until the dough is golden brown at the edges, then sprinkle diced tomato over the flatbread. Cut into strips and serve as an appetizer.

2. If you have a pizza stone, there's no need to pre-bake the dough. Just let the stone heat up in the oven for at least 20 minutes, then place your dressed pizza doughs on it and bake 10-15 minutes.

─── OSTERIA ───

DIAVOLA PIZZAS

SERVES
6 or more

These spicy pizzas are especially good wit freshly-made mozzarella (see page 22), but good-quality storebought mozzarella will also work just fine.

TIME
Total Time: 1 hour (plus time for dough)
Active Time: 25 minutes

INGREDIENTS FOR THE TOMATO SAUCE

2 tablespoons olive oil
1 large yellow onion, diced
8 cloves garlic, minced
1/4 cup (55 grams) tomato paste
1/2 cup (120 mL) red wine
1 1/2 pounds (680 grams) tomatoes, roughly chopped
2 teaspoons salt
1 teaspoon chili flakes
1/2 teaspoon black pepper

FOR THE PIZZA

1 recipe pizza dough, pre-baked (see page 156)
1 large ball mozzarella cheese (see page 22), cut into rounds
4-6 spicy Italian sausages, cut into small pieces
A little olive oil
Freshly ground black pepper
Sprinkle of chili flakes

PREPARATION

1. Preheat the oven to 425F (220C).

2. Make the tomato sauce: In a medium pot, heat the oil. Add the onion and garlic and cook until the onion is translucent, 3-4 minutes. Add the tomato paste and red wine and bring the mixture to a simmer. When the red wine has reduced by half, add the tomatoes, salt, chili flakes, and black pepper. Stir until the tomatoes start to fall apart, then let the sauce simmer, stirring occasionally, for 25-45 minutes. Taste; add salt as needed.

3. Precook the sausages: Heat a little oil in a medium pan and sauté the sausages for 4-6 minutes, until they are evenly browned on all sides.

4. Build the pizza: Spread the tomato sauce to cover your pizza doughs. Place the mozzarella slices evenly around the pizza. Sprinkle the Italian sausages liberally over. Finish with a light drizzle of olive oil and a sprinkle of black pepper and chili flakes.

5. Bake: Bake the pizzas for 8-10 minutes, until both the mozzarella and the sausages are nicely browned.

Sushi Soo

Mr. Kim came for the weather and stayed for the weather. The way he tells it, he first came to Nairobi in 2005 as an importer of an energy drink called Vita500. One morning he woke up and looked out the window and saw the sun shining brightly and in that moment he decided: he wanted to live here. By 2009, his sister and brother-in-law had moved permanently to Kenya and opened a company importing food and equipment from Korea. He decided to shut down the company he'd started in Korea, which helped Koreans to get visas to live and travel abroad, and bring his family to Nairobi. Today he continues to import foods from Korea in partnership with his siblings. They are the only wholesale supplier of Japanese ingredients in Kenya, Tanzania, Rwanda and Uganda.

Mr. Kim loves to eat, and in September 2012, he opened Sushi Soo, a Japanese restaurant. When cooking Japanese food, he said, you're making art, not food. He loves the cuisine for its simplicity and health, and noted that around the world, many Japanese restaurants are owned by Koreans. (This happens to be true in Nairobi, as well.)

He's proud of his ingredients, most of which are imported. For meat, he sources from a farm in Nanyuki that raises grain-fed cows, which he believes to have better marbling than other local beef, the majority of which travel miles a day looking for grass to eat. He's so fanatic about good beef that he imported a fridge for the restaurant specifically for aging meat. He sources tuna, octopus and squid directly from the coast, and claims that they are even better than the seafood in Korea.

When talking to Mr. Kim, his passion and joy for his work were apparent. "I want my restaurant to be like a party where everyone can enjoy together," he exclaimed.

Since he doesn't cook himself, when he opened the restaurant he hired a sushi chef from Dubai by way of the Philippines. Daniel had been working in restaurants in Dubai for eighteen years as a sushi chef, and jumped at the opportunity to move to Kenya. To manage the rest of the kitchen, he hired John Mutuku, who for the previous twenty years had been the head chef at Nihonjin, one of Nairobi's first Japanese restaurants. There he started out as a cleaner and worked his way up under the tutelage of Mr. Sekei, who taught him the intricacies of traditional Japanese food, including how to make traditional ramen from scratch.

Sushi Soo initially opened in a building that they had renovated to include a Korean grocery and a guesthouse. A few months ago they moved to a new location that used to house a Chinese restaurant and before that was a large family home. One small building is now the grocery, and another small building, probably once a shed, houses an adorable Korean bakery. Nairobi sometimes feels like it's changing at lightspeed. Sushi Soo's journey is part of that change, with one immigrant group moving in after another.

~ CHENGDU IMPRESSIONS ~

HUI GUO ROU (TWICE COOKED PORK)

SERVES
3-4

Don't be intimidated by pork belly. This preparation is virtually fool-proof, ensuring that the meat is cooked in the middle and crispy on the outside. If you can't find tianmianjiang, just double the amount of black bean sauce.

TIME
Total Time: 20 minutes
Active Time: 40 minutes

INGREDIENTS

14 ounces (400 grams) pork belly
1 tablespoon neutral oil
1 teaspoon black bean sauce
2 teaspoons minced ginger
2 cloves garlic, very thinly sliced
1 teaspoon sweet wheat paste (tianmianjiang), optional
1 teaspoon soy sauce
1 teaspoon sugar
¼ cup (60 mL) chicken stock
1 large green or yellow pepper, cut into bite-sized pieces
1-2 cups steamed white rice, to serve
Handful of chopped green onions

PREPARATION

1. Boil the pork belly: Place the pork belly in a medium pot and cover it with water. Bring the water to a boil, then reduce the heat to medium-low. Simmer, covered, until the pork is cooked through, about 30 minutes. Remove the pork from the water, let it cool, and then slice it as thinly as you can.

2. Pan-fry the pork belly: Heat the oil in a wok over medium-high heat and add the pork. Cook, stirring, until the pork starts to brown, about 5 minutes.

3. Make the sauce: In a small bowl, whisk together the black bean sauce, ginger, garlic, tianmianjiang, soy sauce, sugar, and stock. Add it to the pan with the pork and cook for about a minute, just until the sauce coats the pork.

4. Cook the pepper: Add the green pepper and cook, stirring, until it is tender and well covered in sauce, about 5 minutes. Taste; add salt or soy sauce to your liking.

5. Serve: Serve with steamed rice and a sprinkle of chopped green onions.

~~~ PURDY ARMS ~~~

BEEF BURGER

YIELD
8 burgers

The burgers are Purdy Arms are a Nairobi institution. Served with fries and sweet, crunchy coleslaw, it's a meal that leaves you happily stuffed.

TIME
Total Time: 20 minutes
Active Time: 20 minutes

INGREDIENTS FOR THE BURGER PATTIES

2 1/4 pounds (1 kg) minced beef
1 egg
2 medium onions, minced
1 bunch parsley, finely chopped
1/2 cup (about 60 grams) bread crumbs
2 tablespoons dijon mustard
1/4 cup (60 mL) neutral oil, plus a little more for cooking
Pinch of salt per burger

TO SERVE

8 hamburger buns, halved
A little melted butter
3 tomatoes, sliced
Handful iceberg lettuce leaves
Mayonnaise, mustard, and other condiments, to your liking
1 cup caramelized onions (see recipe on page 166)

PREPARATION

1. Make the hamburger meat: In a large bowl, mix together all the patty ingredients. Form 8 patties, making them slightly thinner in the middle than at the edges, and taking care to make them just slightly bigger in diameter than the buns.

2. Cook: Heat a very thin layer of oil in a large pan over medium-high heat. Place four patties in the hot pan. Sprinkle salt over them and cook for three minutes on the first side. Flip, sprinkle a bit more salt, and cook three minutes more on the second side. This will yield a nice rare burger. For medium rare, cook four minutes on each side; for medium, five.

3. Construct: Brush the cut sides of the hamburger buns with a little melted butter. Lightly toast the hamburger buns in a very hot pan. Stack the burger with the condiments and vegetables of your choice, topping it off with a mound of caramelized onions (page 166). Enjoy with a side of green apple slaw (page 63).

NOTES

If you make your own bread crumbs, as The Purdy Arms does, then don't be afraid to let them get a little extra toasted in the oven. A touch of char in the breadcrumbs is a nice stand in for the flavor imparted to burgers by a grill.

~ PURDY ARMS ~

CARAMELIZED ONIONS

YIELD
about 1 1/2 cups

TIME
Total Time: 45 minutes
Active Time: 25 minutes

INGREDIENTS
2 1/4 pounds (1 kg) yellow onions, sliced
2 tablespoons neutral oil
1/3 cup (80 mL) balsamic vinegar
1/4 cup (50 grams) brown sugar
Salt, to taste

PREPARATION

1. Brown the onions: Heat the oil in a large skillet over high heat. Add the onions; they should sizzle. Cook the onions, turning them every 3 minutes or so, until they are starting to brown, about 10 minutes.

2. Lower the heat to medium. Cook the onions for 10 more minutes; they should be noticeably reduced in size.

3. Caramelize: Add the brown sugar and the balsamic vinegar. Stir to coat all of the onions. With the heat still low, continue to cook the onions, stirring occasionally, until there is no excess liquid in the pan, 15-20 minutes more. The onions should be very dark brown and extremely soft. Add a pinch of salt and let the onions cool to room temperature.

4. Serve: Place a mound of caramelized onions atop burgers (see page 164).

Bodyzone

Sisters Irene Tekiendwa and Veronica (Bianca) Nyangai were born on the Kenyan coast, but both found themselves pulled to Europe and then Congo. Irene worked for eight years as a flight attendant for Kenya Airways, traveling the world, but always coming home to Kenya. Bianca studied hotel management and built a career in hospitality, working for hotels and restaurants in East Africa. Irene married a Congolese man, and in 2012, they opened Bodyzone in Nairobi's Kilimani neighborhood. By then, both she and Bianca spoke fluent Lingala, and also a bit of French.

Walking into the Bodyzone compound, you first see a garden filled with round tables hidden under large umbrellas and experience the smell of grilling fish wafting from the kitchen. The restaurant serves primarily Congolese food, but attracts a clientele from all over the continent, especially West Africa. At any moment you'll hear French, Swahili, English and Lingala being spoken. Walking past the restaurant area, you'll encounter the spa, where you can get a manicure or massage with your meal. Continue past the spa and you'll see a garage where mechanics repair cars. There's also a carwash and shisha lounge further down. This restaurant is truly full-service.

During the day, the restaurant is filled with people from nearby offices, traveling businessmen catching up with clients, and politicians holding working lunches. In the evening, the restaurant transforms into a thumping lounge, loud music playing as the same customers who came for lunch unwind and catch up with friends. There's bottle service and private rooms for those looking for privacy, and for everyone else, there are comfy couches and garden seating. On Sundays, Congolese bands play live music.

The chefs are Congolese and the food they prepare is inspired by Lake Kivu. Almost everyone orders fish, and the big question is grilled or stewed. It's best to visit with a group and order both versions since they're delicious and enormous! The grilled version is smoked over hot coals, creating a crackly crisp skin and a hint of smokiness in the meat. Doused in lemon juice, it's perfect with rice or fried plantains. The stewed version is similar prepared, but then slow cooked in a stew strikingly reminiscent of romesco sauce, rich and silky, and delicious with fufu, a thick cassava porridge, and pondu, a cassava leaf stew.

Back when Bodyzone opened four years ago, they were the only restaurant serving West and Central African cuisine. Today, Bianca says, there's competition, but they all fill different niches. Nairobi is constantly evolving as people come and go, and the food scene is indisputably influenced, and improved, by these changes.

š

~ TASTE OF JAMAICA ~

MEAT PATTIES

SERVES
8 large patties

Think of these meat patties as oversized beef samosas, dressed up with the flavors of curry powder, thyme, and hot pepper.

TIME
Total Time: 1 hour
Active Time: 45 minutes

INGREDIENTS FOR THE PASTRY
2 cups (260 grams) all-purpose flour
1/2 teaspoon salt
1/2 teaspoon curry powder
1/2 cup (114 grams) chilled butter
1/3 cup + 2 tablespoons (110 mL) ice water
1 egg + 1/4 cup (60 mL) water

FOR THE MEAT FILLING
2 tablespoons neutral oil
1 white onion, finely chopped
1/2 hot pepper, minced
18 ounces (500 grams) ground beef
1/2 teaspoon salt
1/2 teaspoon ground black pepper
1/2 teaspoon curry powder
1/2 teaspoon dried thyme
1/4 cup (60 mL) beef or chicken stock
1/4 cup (about 30 grams) dry breadcrumbs

PREPARATION

1. Make the pastry: Combine the flour, curry powder, and salt in a large bowl. Use a cheese grater to grate the chilled butter into the flour mixture. Toss the butter in the flour with your fingers. Add the ice water and use a spatula to stir. When the dough is moist, with just a few dry crumbs remaining, turn it onto a clean work surface and knead gently until the dough comes together. (At this point, you can refrigerate the dough until you're ready to use it, up to 24 hours; simply let it warm to room temperature for 15 minutes before using it.)

2. Make the meat filling: In a large pan over medium-high heat, heat the oil. Add the onion and hot pepper and sauté until they are limp, 2-3 minutes. Add the ground beef, salt, pepper, curry powder, and thyme and stir. Brown the meat for about 10 minutes, stirring from time to time. Add the stock and the breadcrumbs and stir until no excess liquid remains in the pan, 2-3 minutes. Remove the skillet from the heat and let the filling cool while you roll out the dough.

3. Build the patties: Preheat the oven to 400F (200C). Divide the dough into two balls. Roll the first ball into a large rectangle about 1/16-inch thick. Press a plate with approximately a 6-inch diameter into the dough to draw the outlines of circles. Use a knife or a pizza cutter to cut out the circles; gather up the scraps and continue with the rest of the dough, until you have 8 circles of pastry.

4. Make the egg wash: In a small bowl, whisk together the egg and 1/4 cup water. Set aside.

5. Build the pastries: Use a 1/3 cup measure to scoop filling onto one half of each dough circle, leaving a 1/2-inch border at the edges. Brush a little water around the edge of the circle and fold the circle in half. Use a fork to press the edges together. Brush the egg wash over the pastry and poke a couple of holes in the tops of the pastries to release steam.

6. Cook: Place the meat patties onto lightly greased baking sheets. Bake until the patties are browned on top and bottom, about 10 minutes; switch the oven position of the sheets halfway through. Let the patties cool for about 5 minutes before serving.

NOTES

Scotch Bonnet peppers are the hot pepper of choice in this recipe. If they are available to you, use just 1/4 of one—about 1/4 teaspoon when minced—as they are quite strong.

CHEKA

CHICKEN TERIYAKI

SERVES
4-6

Cheka's delicious chicken teriyaki hits the perfect balance between sweet and umami flavors. Served with a handful of crunchy carrot and cabbage salad, it makes either a perfect appetizer for a larger group or a great main for 4 or more. It can easily be scaled up to serve a large party.

TIME
Total Time: 30 minutes
Active Time: 30 minutes

INGREDIENTS
6 boneless chicken thighs, with skin (each about 5 ounces/150 grams)
4 tablespoons neutral oil, divided
¼ cup (60 mL) soy sauce
¼ cup (60 mL) mirin

TO SERVE
½ cup (50 grams) grated carrot
½ cup (60 grams) grated cabbage
about 2 cups cooked white rice

PREPARATION

1. Cook the chicken: Heat 2 tablespoons oil over medium high heat in a large pan. Place three chicken thighs, skin side down, in the pan. (Be careful; they may splatter a bit in the oil.) Cook for about 5 minutes, until the skin is nicely browned. Flip the thighs over and cook for an additional 3-5 minutes. Remove one piece from the pan and make a small cut into its thickest part. If it's cooked through, remove the chicken from the pan and place on a cutting board to cool. If it's still pink, cook for 3-5 minutes more before setting the chicken aside. Do the same with the remaining oil and chicken thighs.

2. Prepare the teriyaki sauce: While the chicken is cooling, combine the soy sauce, mirin, and sake in a medium bowl.

3. Cut the chicken into strips: Use a very sharp knife to cut the cooled chicken into strips about one inch thick. Place the strips back in the pan, put the heat to medium, and pour the teriyaki sauce over the chicken. Cook for 2-4 minutes, until the teriyaki sauce has thickened
slightly and coated the chicken.

4. Serve: Serve the teriyaki chicken over rice, spooning the extra teriyaki sauce over. Garnish with a small handful of grated cabbage and carrots, for crunch.

NOTES

If you're making teriyaki chicken for a large group, you can do steps 1 and 2 ahead of time. Then, at mealtime, all you have to do is cut the chicken into strips and cook it briefly in the teriyaki sauce.

Little Sheep Hot Pot

The first time I experienced Little Sheep Hot Pot was by accident. I was new to Nairobi, having just arrived a month before, and one day while driving by noticed big red paper lanterns hanging outside and figured (hopefully) it must be a Chinese restaurant. With some friends I ventured down the long muddy drive way and arrived at a house surrounded by a lush garden and huge trees. Sure enough, the smells of chili oil and bone broth wafted out as we wandered in. A few tables with booths were scattered around the living room, and a family was sitting down for dinner. Upon seeing us, an older man and woman jumped up and quickly welcomed us in and guided us to a table. They were the owners and we were apparently among their first clients. From then on, Little Sheep Hot Pot became a staple in my life, kind of a beacon, a place where I go when I want a taste of home, or just to be around people who like my family, feed me, then tell me I'm losing too much weight and have to eat more, or am gaining weight and should exercise, and are just genuinely happy to see me.

Mr. and Mrs. Pai ended up in Nairobi on a fluke. They moved to Burundi in 1992 from Jiangsu to set up a textile factory. They'd never been to Africa; they were small business owners in China and wanted to try their luck at a new and better life. They operated the textile factory for two years until political instability in Burundi caused them to leave. In the Nairobi airport during a layover, they met a Tawainese couple who told them that how happy they were in Kenya, so they decided to stay. They eventually found work in construction and in importing and exporting.

Many of the immigrants who we've featuring have started families here and established roots, and Mr. and Mrs. Pai are no different. Their son is now married to a Filipina woman of Chinese descent (who doesn't speak Chinese), and they have two sons who were born in Nairobi and attend an international school where they speak English. Their lingua franca is English, despite Mr. and Mrs. Pai's clear preference for Mandarin – so much so that many of their staff speak and understand Chinese.

In 2013 they decided that they wanted to open a restaurant. Mrs. Pai is vivacious and outgoing, a natural hostess. In opening the restaurant, she wanted to create a space where people could socialize and meet each other, sort of like a community center. Many of their early customers were Chinese, but very quickly the novelty of the restaurant started attracting people of all nationalities.

The restaurant itself is a sprawling house where the downstairs has been converted into dining areas, small tables and booths are spread across the living room, and big round tables are squeezed into the dining room and patio. A stairway in the center of the dining room separates the restaurant from the family home. It's not unusual to see Mr. and Mrs. Pai's grandchildren playing videogames in the middle of the living room, or running around outside or jumping on the trampoline. All of the rooms are covered in a pastelly, flowery wallpaper, shade and style evoking trendy vintage dresses that might equally be worn by a hipster or a grandmother in a 1980's romcom. Some walls display large Chinese fans draped in colorful sequined boas while other walls are decked in Christmas lights arranged in shapes like a heart or a flower. Tables are covered in white crocheted doilies, some plastic others cotton, which somehow remain perpetually stainless. From the ceilings in all the rooms hang rainbow streamers, giving the feeling that it's eternally a birthday party at Christmas time in a Chinese grandmother's house.

Needless to say, for many, in addition to the Pai family, it is home.

~~~ FOGO GAUCHO ~~~

STEAK SKEWERS

 SERVES
150 grams of meat will be enough for one. Multiply it to suit your party.

Fogo Gaucho is proud of the fact that nothing but meat and salt - no fancy rubs or marinades - go into their delicious steak skewers. For that reason, using high-quality, lightly marbled meat with enough fat to render in a hot pan is key to a good result.

 TIME
Total Time: 15 minutes
Active Time: 15 minutes

 SPECIAL TOOLS
Wooden skewers

 INGREDIENTS
5 ounces (140 grams) sirloin or rump steak per person
Sprinkle of salt

 PREPARATION

1. Prepare your skewers: Soak the skewers in water for at least 10 minutes.

2. Prepare the meat: Trim nerves and rough parts of the meat, leaving the fat on. Sprinkle the cuts of meat with salt and cut into 6-8 chunks (about 20 grams each).

3. Cook the meat: Skewer the meat, making sure that the fat side of each piece is on the same side. Bring a grill or a heavy-bottomed pan to very high heat; don't add any oil. Place your skewers in the hot pan or grill, fat side down, and sear until the fat is nicely browned and starting to render, about 3 minutes. Rotate the skewers 180 degrees and cook another minute for rare, or 2 minutes for medium.

NOTES

Sirloin and rump steak both work wonderfully for this dish. Sirloin tends to have a more classically meaty taste, while rump steak is a bit more tender. Try both and find out your preference; or, mix the two cuts on a single skewer.

Purdy Arms

Nairobi's Karen neighborhood is located on the south edge of the city, bordering the Nairobi National Park (the only game park in the world located inside a major city's limits) and the picturesque Ngong Hills, made famous in the book *Out of Africa*. Down the street from the Karen Blixen Museum, the eponymous former house of the author of *Out of Africa*, is Purdy Arms, a beautiful pub sitting on twenty-five acres of forest.

The building where Purdy Arms now resides had many lives before becoming a pub. It was built in the 1950s by an architect who designed it for his own family. The single-story house had sweeping views of the surrounding forest and a swimming pool. He later sold the house to the Purdy family, who then relocated to England and left the house completely dilapidated. The Catholic Church then came in and bought the property. In the early 2000s, the church rented it to a woman named Ms. Leggit, who turned it into a drug rehabilitation center. Jules Sandy-Lumsdaine used to attend Alcoholics Anonymous meetings there. When Jules and her husband, Rob Davidson, closed their former pub, the Rusty Nail, in 2013, they took over the building and reopened it as Purdy Arms.

Rob is the finance director for a local airline, but his passion is rugby, so when he and Jules decided to open Purdy Arms, they designed it to be a sports bar where people could go for a pint, watch a game, and eat some really good food – pub grub with a twist. Jules describes the growth of the bar into a restaurant and B&B as an accident; the additions came with customer demand. Jules is third-generation British Kenyan: her grandfather arrived when Kenya was still a British colony. She studied business administration and worked for the Kenya Flower Council before becoming an accidental restaurateur when, thirteen years ago, her husband bought a bar called the Outside Inn to be his hobby. Jules grew up around really good food; her mother was a Cordon Bleu-trined chef. Today, she calls the restaurant a "crockpot of creativity," where her chefs are constantly experimenting with new flavors and techniques. She proudly gives her chefs space to be creative, and that's how they've ended up with dishes like chicken tikka salad, which melds Kenya's British cuisine with Indian.

Jules is bursting with energy and Purdy Arms is a place where she can indulge her passion for food with her passion for people. She seems to know every customer who walks in personally, and she takes time to catch up with each one. She's also committed to giving back to the community, hosting fundraisers at the restaurant and opening it up as an outing for local children's homes. Several of her employees, including a sous chef, are HIV positive, a hiring choice that she made conscientiously, understanding that she could provide an opportunity for those individuals and be an example to others.

Despite its British heritage, Purdy Arms has integrated aspects of Kenyan culture, Kenyan immigrant culture, and British immigrant culture. Every Sunday they have a curry buffet, which originated among South Asian communities on the coast. It grew to be part of the wider Kenyan culture on the coast, and now Purdy's has adapted it for a Nairobi clientele, many of whom are British transplants who grew up eating curries in England.

The restaurant combines traditions with a deft touch, exemplifying how old immigrant communities can embrace the new.

~~~ SUSHI SOO ~~~

PORK KATSUDON

SERVES
4

Sushi Soo deep fries the pork that goes into their pork katsudon, which is, it goes without saying, delicious. for a slightly healthier home version, we cook the pork cutlets in a skillet with just a small amount of oil. As long as you select high quality, lightly marbled pork, the home result will be just as delicious.

TIME
Total Time: 40 minutes
Active Time: 40 minutes

INGREDIENTS FOR THE PORK
4 pieces pork loin (5 ounces/150 grams each)
Salt & pepper
3⁄4 cup (190 grams) tempura flour (see note)
2 eggs, lightly beaten
1 cup (about 130 grams) panko breadcrumbs
2 tablespoons neutral oil, for frying

FOR THE SAUCE
3/4 cup (180 mL) soy sauce
2 tablespoons granulated sugar
3 tablespoons water
1/3 cup (80 mL) mirin (or other rice wine)
1 tablespoon freshly grated ginger

FOR THE RICE BOWL
2 tablespoons neutral oil
2 medium yellow onions, thinly sliced
4 eggs, lightly beaten
2 cups (340 grams) cooked white rice
Green onions and sesame seeds, to garnish

PREPARATION

1. **Prepare the meat:** Sprinkle both sides of the meat with salt and pepper and rub it in with your fingers. Then, use a meat pounder or a heavy rolling pin to flatten the meat to a thickness of 1/2 inch.

2. **Prepare the breading:** Set out three bowls and fill one with the tempura flour, one with the lightly beaten eggs, and the third with the panko breadcrumbs.

3. **Cook the pork:** Heat the oil in a large pan over medium heat. Dredge the pork cutlets in the tempura flour, then the egg, then the breadcrumbs. Set the cutlets in the heated pan, being sure not to crowd them. Cover the pan with a lid and cook the pork for 5 minutes on the first side. Flip and cook, uncovered, for an additional 5 minutes. Then, remove a cutlet and make a small cut into the middle to see that it's no longer pink. If it is, continue cooking the pork for another 2-3 minutes. (Or, use an instant-read thermometer to check that the meat has reached an internal temperature of 145F/63C.) If it's white all the way through, remove the pork from the pan and set on a cutting board to cool.

4. **Make the sauce:** Combine all the sauce ingredients in a small bowl. Whisk until the sugar dissolves.

5. **Slice the pork:** Once the cutlets are cool enough to handle, cut them them into slices about as fat as your little finger.

6. **Cook the vegetables:** Heat 2 more tablespoons oil in a large pan over medium-high heat. Fry the onions until they are translucent, about 3 minutes. Pour 3⁄4 cup (180 mL) sauce over and stir until the onions are well coated. Add the 4 beaten eggs and cook, stirring gently, until they are no longer runny, about 2 minutes. Turn off the heat.

7. **Plate:** Divide the rice evenly into four bowls. Scoop the egg/onion mixture over the rice and top with slices of pork. Drizzle the remaining sauce over and garnish with chopped green onions and a sprinkle of sesame seeds.

NOTES

1. You can make your own tempura flour by simply mixing ¾ cup white (100 grams) flour with 2 tablespoons cornstarch.
2. Don't let a lack of panko keep you from making this recipe: you can easily make your own panko-style breadcrumbs! Simply cut a day-old baguette or half loaf of sandwich bread into thick slices and toast them in a warm oven (about 300F/150C) until they are lightly browned. Crumble them by hand or in a food processor, leaving some pea-sized crumbs in the mix.
3. To make a vegetarian version of this recipe, you can replace the pork with eggplant or tofu steaks, if desired. Simply cut the eggplant or tofu into inch-thick rounds, then dredge and cook in the same way as the pork.

~~~ TRATTORIA ~~~

PASTA CARBONARA

SERVES
4

Luna introduces this dish with a disclaimer: there's no one way to make carbonara. The recipe will change from household to household in Rome, the city the pasta calls home . . . and even within her own family. Her father likes to add cream to his carbonara, but she is passionately against it. We've shared her recipe here, but feel free to make it your own!

TIME
Total Time: 15 minutes
Active Time: 15 minutes

INGREDIENTS
14 ounces (400 grams) dry spaghetti noodles
3 egg yolks
½ cup (60 grams) pecorino cheese, finely grated
4 ounces (115 grams) guanciale (pork cheek), pancetta, or bacon, cubed
1 tablespoon olive oil
Pinch of salt and black pepper

PREPARATION

1. Boil the pasta: Bring a large pot of generously salted water to boil. Add the spaghetti and cook until al dente, about 8 minutes. Strain the pasta and set it aside, reserving about 1 cup (240 mL) of the cooking water.

2. Prepare the eggs & cheese: In a small bowl, whisk together the egg yolks and half of the grated pecorino. Add a pinch each of salt and pepper. Set the eggs aside.

3. Sauté the guanciale: Heat a medium pan over high heat and add the olive oil. Add the cubed guanciale and turn down the heat to medium. Cook, stirring, until the meat is brown and crispy, about 10 minutes. If the pan becomes too dry and looks like it's going to burn, add a splash of white wine, stock, or water.

4. Put it together: With the heat still on, add the cooked pasta to the guanciale and stir to coat the pasta in the rendered fat. Turn off the heat and add the egg mixture to the pasta, stirring well to coat the pasta. If the pasta seems too thick, add in a little of the cooking water (Trattoria skips this step, but it's useful if your carbonara isn't coming out as creamy as you'd like it). Taste; add salt and pepper to your liking.

5. Serve: Divide the pasta into serving bowls and garnish with the remaining pecorino and a sprinkle of parsley.

~~~ FOGO GAUCHO ~~~

FEIJOADA

 **SERVES** 6

Featuring sausage, bacon, shank, *and* pancetta, this dish is a dream come true for pork lovers.

 TIME
Total Time: 30 minutes
Active Time: 1.5 hours, plus soaking time

 INGREDIENTS
1 ¼ cup (280 grams) dry black beans
1 link smoked pork sausage
4 slices thick-cut bacon
6 ounces (170 grams) pork knee or shank
3.5 ounces (100 grams) pancetta
1 large yellow onion, chopped
5 cloves garlic, minced
1 tablespoon salt
2 cups (480 mL) low-sodium chicken stock, plus extra water as needed
½ cup (30 grams) chopped parsley
Cooked white rice, to serve

 PREPARATION

1. Soak the beans: Wash the beans well; soak them overnight or for at least 12 hours. Strain the beants out of the soaking liquid and set them aside.

2. Brown the pork: Cut all the pork meats into very small chunks. Place the meat in a large, heavy-bottomed pot and bring it to medium-high heat. The fat on the meat will begin to render; after 3-4 minutes, turn the meat to brown on the other side. (If you find that the meat is sticking, it may be because the pork is not quite fatty enough; add a tablespoon of neutral oil to help the pork brown.)

3. Simmer: Add the onion, garlic, and salt and cook until the onions are translucent, 2-3 minutes. Add the soaked black beans and the chicken stock and stir. If the stock doesn't quite cover the meat and the beans, add a bit of water. Simmer, uncovered, over low heat for about 1 hour, until most of the liquid has evaporated and the beans are tender.

4. Garnish and serve: Stir the chopped parsley into the beans and add salt to taste. Serve feijoada over rice.

NOTES
If you find you can never plan ahead enough to pre-soak dry beans, don't despair: in a pinch, you can swap in 14 ounces / 400 grams canned black beans.

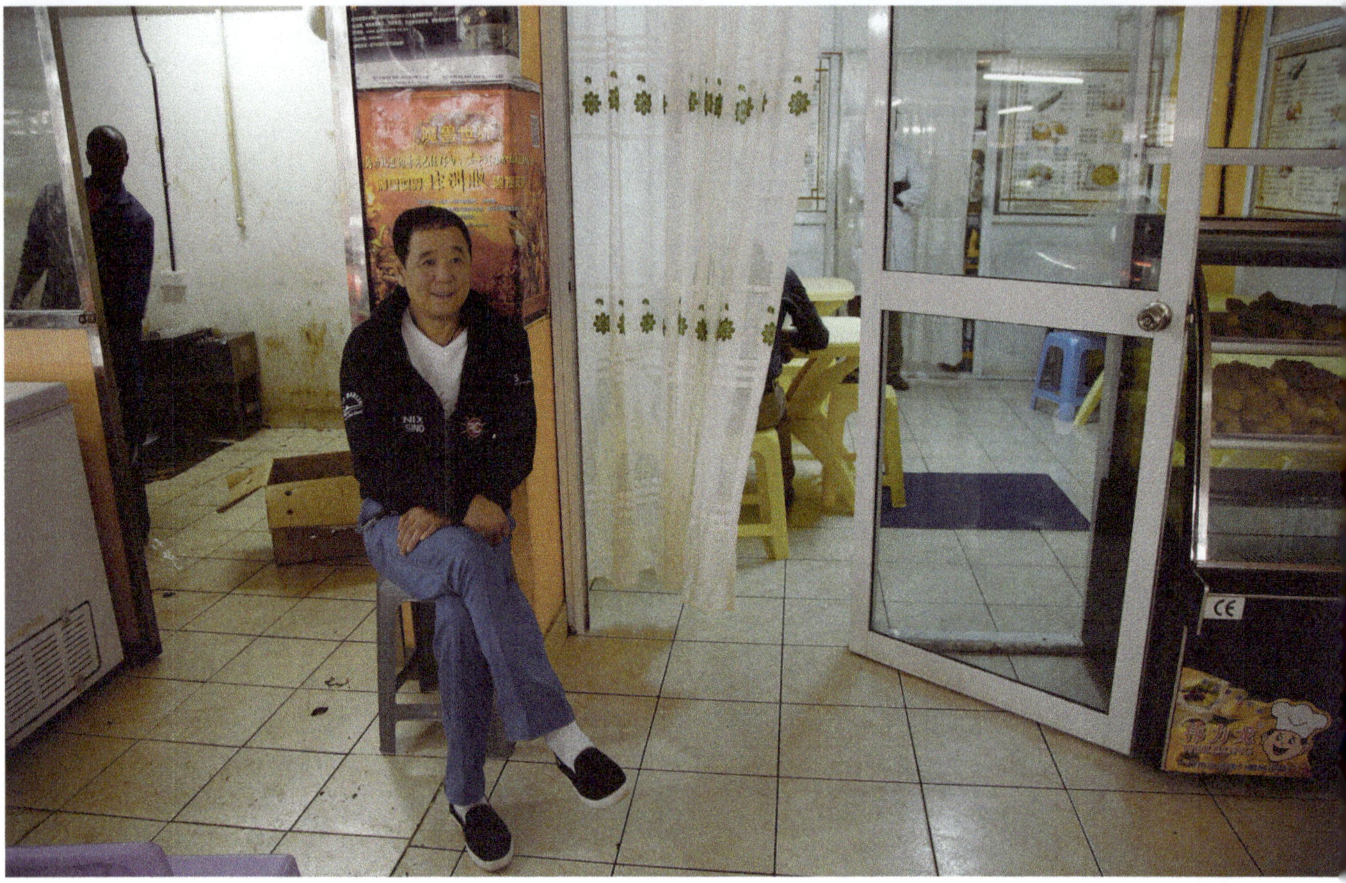
CE

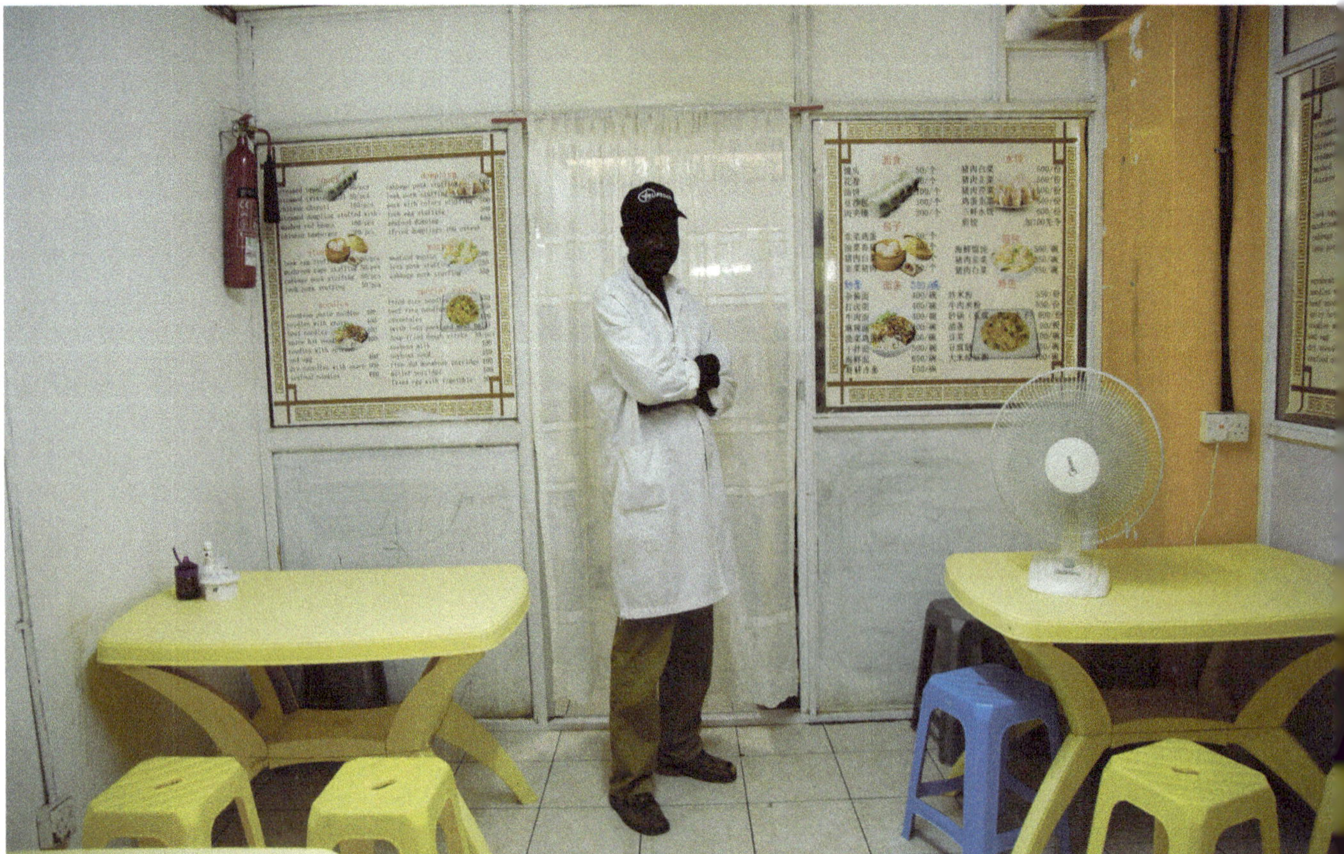

Cailan Caoshi

Four and a half years ago, when I first moved here, I used to buy Chinese groceries out of a garage hidden behind a shopping mall called the China Center. Inside the China Center were a variety of shops, including a dry goods store that gave out loyalty cards and had a monthly raffle (I once won shrimp chips!) and an Ethiopian restaurant. The garage wasn't always open, but on the weekends it was a good bet that you'd be able to get fresh produce and pork butchered to order. One day, the shop disappeared and resurfaced months later a few blocks away in the basement of an office building. Less hidden this time and in a street-facing location, the Cai Lan Supermarket is filled to the brim with locally-grown Chinese produce and imported dry goods.

Descending the ramp into the market from the parking lot feels like stepping into a vortex that drops you in the middle of a Chinese market street. From all sides you hear people shouting, produce being tossed from one aisle to another, old people serenely picking through piles of greens, cleavers breaking down all manner of meats, and children and animals running underfoot. Little is surprising here, even a crab scurrying across the floor hoping not to be someone's dinner.

Amidst the chaos, behind a lace curtain, is a little restaurant serving ridiculously delicious fresh dumplings, noodles and steamed buns. The décor is simple: four plastic tables with four plastic stools each and big menus taped up in both English and Chinese. There's a glass display case in front filled with buns to go. The kitchen consists of a double gas burner, some cutting boards, and a small fridge. The staff squeezed in the kitchen are an older Chinese man, Mr. Gao Xian Ang, always with a cigarette hanging from his lips, a Kenyan cook who speaks Chinese, and a waitress.

Mr. Gao moved to Nairobi in 2000 from Harbin, the capital of China's northernmost province. There he'd worked in numerous restaurants and learned to make noodles, various types of dumplings, and buns from scratch.

His younger sister and older brother had come to Kenya even earlier, in 1998, importing Chinese goods and selling them here. He quickly got into the souvenir business and made bags that he sold to local shops. He ran this business for seven years before deciding to open a restaurant, called Harbin, which he later sold to another Chinese entrepreneur. In 2011 he moved to South Sudan, where he worked in a hotel, but after two years decided to come back to Nairobi. When he returned, he decided to return to the restaurant business, and acquired a small space in the supermarket to open his little shop, where his staff now churns out those delicious noodles, dumplings, and buns.

When asked if he plans to stay here long term, he nodded gruffly and commented that the weather here is good. This makes all the more sense when you consider that the province he comes from is located in Siberia and has an average temperature of 0 degrees Fahrenheit (-18 degrees Celsius) in the winter. His children are in China still, but he's built a life in Nairobi where he has a business, opportunities and community.

~ AFGHAN HOUSE ~

MUTTON SHORVA

 SERVES
6

 TIME
Total Time: 3 hours
Active Time: 30 Min

 SPECIAL TOOLS
Slow cooker

 INGREDIENTS
2.2 pounds (1 kilogram) mutton, cut into bite-sized cubes
4 tablespoons neutral oil
2 yellow onions, finely chopped
1 teaspoon black pepper
4 whole cardamom pods, crushed
1 teaspoon cumin powder
½ teaspoon turmeric powder
½ teaspoon black pepper
½ tablespoon minced ginger
½ tablespoon minced garlic
½ teaspoon salt
2 cups (480 mL) chicken stock
6 green chilies, halved
½ teaspoon allspice powder
Cooked white rice and/or naan, to serve

 PREPARATION

1. Boil the mutton: Place the cubed mutton in a slow cooker, cover it with water, and cook over very low heat for 2 hours. Remove the meat from the water and set it aside.

2. Make the spice paste: In a large pan, heat the oil. Add the onions and cook until they're translucent, 2-3 minutes. Add the cardamom, cumin, turmeric, black pepper, ginger, garlic, and salt.

3. Simmer: Add the mutton and fry until the meat is well coated with the spices. Add the chicken stock and the green chilies, bring the liquid to a boil, then reduce the heat and simmer, uncovered, for 20-30 minutes. Add the allspice powder. Remove the chilies and the cardamom pods from the stew. Taste; add salt and pepper to your liking.

4. Serve: Serve mutton shorva over rice, with a side of bread.

~

"Settling is not easy.
At some point, you
have to be strong
enough to say,
now."

Gaetano, Trattoria

~

Fish & Seafood Mains

192	MOQUECA OF PRAWNS	Fogo Gaucho
194	CATERPILLAR SUSHI	Furusato
196	BEAN STEW WITH PLANTAINS	Mama Ashanti
200	GRILLED SALMON	Misono
202	DYNAMITE FUTO MAKI ROLL	Sushi Soo
204	TAKUWAN (PICKLED DIAKON RADISH)	Sushi Soo
208	SEAFOOD MARMITE	Table 49
210	SAMAKI MOSHI	Bodyzone
212	SAUCE POISSON (NILE PERCH WITH RED PEPPER SAUCE)	Bodyzone
214	CRAB & GINGER PASTA	Trattoria

FOGO GAUCHO

MOQUECA OF PRAWNS

SERVES
4-6

This creamy soup comes together remarkably quickly, and is infinitely adaptable: you can swap in shrimp or chicken for the prawns and sugar snap peas or French beans in place of one of the sweet sweet peppers. The key is the creamy, very slightly tart broth and plenty of fresh cilantro.

TIME
Total Time: 40 Min
Active Time: 30 Min

PREPARATION

1. **Marinate the prawns:** Toss the prawns with the lemon juice, garlic, and white pepper. Let sit for 20 minutes.

2. **Sauté:** Heat the oils over high heat in a wok or a large, deep skillet. Sauté the sliced onions until they begin to brown, then add the peppers and cook for three minutes. Add the prawns, with their marinade, and cook until they start to turn pink, about three minutes.

3. **Simmer:** Add the tomatoes, coconut milk, and salt and reduce the heat to medium. Simmer for about 8 minutes, until the prawns are opaque.

4. **Serve:** Just before serving, stir in the fresh cilantro. Taste; add salt if needed. Serve over rice.

INGREDIENTS

2 ¼ pounds (1 kg) prawns, peeled & cleaned
2 tablespoons lemon juice
6 cloves garlic, finely minced
½ teaspoon white pepper
1 tablespoon palm oil
1 tablespoon canola oil
1 onion, thinly sliced
1 green pepper, 1 red pepper, and 1 yellow pepper, all seeded and thinly sliced
3 medium tomatoes, roughly chopped
2 14-oz tins (800 mL) coconut milk
1 teaspoon salt, plus more to taste
Small bunch of cilantro, chopped
2 cups cooked rice

~ FOGO GAUCHO ~

CATERPILLAR SUSHI

MAKES
6 rolls

This maki roll is inspired by some of the most common fruits in Kenya: mango and avocado. It also has a generous amount of mayonnaise, which is a standard ingredient in Nairobi sushi. Feel free to adjust it to your liking.

TIME
Total Time: 2 hours
Active Time: 20 minutes

INGREDIENTS

2 cups (400 grams) uncooked sushi rice

3 cups (720 mL) water

¼ cup (60 mL) rice vinegar

2 tablespoons sugar

½ teaspoon salt

2 large cucumbers, sliced into long pieces

1 mango, peeled, pitted, and thinly sliced

1 avocado, peeled, pitted & thinly sliced

18 ounces (500 grams) crab sticks (optional)

¼ cup (55 grams) mayonnaise

1 tablespoon sriracha or other hot sauce

6 sheets of seaweed (nori)

Soy sauce, wasabi, and pickled ginger, for serving

PREPARATION

1. Make the sushi rice: Rinse the rice in water three times: the water should run clear. Then, combine the rice and water in a medium saucepan, bring to a boil, and simmer until the water is absorbed and the rice is tender, about 12 minutes.

2. In a small saucepan, combine the rice vinegar, sugar, and salt. Simmer until the sugar and salt dissolve.

3. Transfer the cooked rice into a mixing bowl. Pour the vinegar mixture over and stir to coat well. Let the rice cool completely.

4. Make the spicy mayo: Combine the mayonnaise and chili paste, adjusting spiciness to your liking, in a small bowl.

5. Construct: Lay a sheet of nori on a sushi rolling mat or a slightly damp kitchen towel. Cover the seaweed with a layer of rice, leaving 1/2-inch of seaweed uncovered at the top. Press down firmly on the rice (dipping your fingers in water first will help keep the rice from sticking to you). Dab a line of chili mayonnaise across the top of the rectangle, then place two strips each of cucumber, mango, avocado, and crab on top. Starting at the top edge, roll the sushi down, using your hands to keep it pressed closed. When you get to the bottom, brush the nori with a little water to help it adhere. Continue in the same way until you run out of ingredients.

6. Cut and serve: Use a very sharp knife to cut your rolls into slices. Serve with soy sauce, wasabi, and pickled ginger, if desired.

~ MAMA ASHANTI ~

BEAN STEW WITH PLANTAINS

SERVES
4-6

This bean stew is not the world's most beautiful dish, but it is delicious. The salty smokiness of the fish is perfectly balanced by the sweetness of fried plantains.

TIME
Total Time: 45 minutes
Active Time: 45 minutes

INGREDIENTS FOR THE STEW
1 tablespoon neutral oil
2 medium yellow onions, minced
6-8 tomatoes, roughly chopped
1 teaspoon salt
2 teaspoons curry powder
7 ounces (200 grams) smoked fish
2 ½ cups (425 grams) cooked kidney beans

FOR THE PLANTAINS
3 ripe plantains (or more, if you'd like to have extra for snacking on)
1 cup (240 mL) cooking oil (palm, sunflower, canola, or a mix)

PREPARATION

1. Make the stew base: Heat the oil in a large pot over medium-high heat. Add the onions and cook, stirring, for 2-3 minutes. Add the tomatoes, salt, and curry powder and reduce the heat to medium. Simmer the tomatoes, stirring occasionally, until they break down, about 10 minutes.

2. Prepare the fish & beans: While the tomato sauce is simmering, cut the fish into bite-size pieces. Place 1 ¼ cups of the kidney beans into the bowl of a food processor and pulse until they are thoroughly blended; the mixture will have a texture somewhere between a paste and a powder.

3. Combine: Add the remaining whole beans and the fish to the tomato base and stir to combine. Stir in the mashed beans and reduce the heat to low. Simmer, stirring occasionally to ensure the stew doesn't stick to the bottom of the pot, for 10-15 minutes, until it is quite thick. Taste and add salt if needed. (Be sure to taste a bite with fish in it, as the fish gives the stew much of its saltiness.)

4. Fry the plantains: While the stew is thickening, heat 1 cup oil in a medium pan over high heat. (If your pan is more than 10" in diameter, add a bit of extra oil.) Peel the plantains and cut them into rounds about as thick as your little finger. Carefully place the rounds in the oil. After about 3 minutes, flip one over. If it has turned a deep golden brown, flip all the rounds and cook for about 3 minutes more, until they are nicely browned on both sides. (Exact cooking time depends on your pan and the ripeness of the plantains, so keep an eye on the plantains, flipping a couple of pieces frequently, to make sure they don't burn.) Transfer the cooked plantains to a paper towel-lined plate and sprinkle them with salt.

5. Serve: Serve large bowls of stew with a generous handful of fried plantains.

NOTES

When choosing your plantains for this dish, opt for ones that are nice and ripe. The skin should be speckled with brown and they should be a bit tender to the touch. And it goes without saying: fried plantains make a delicious snack on their own, no bean stew required.

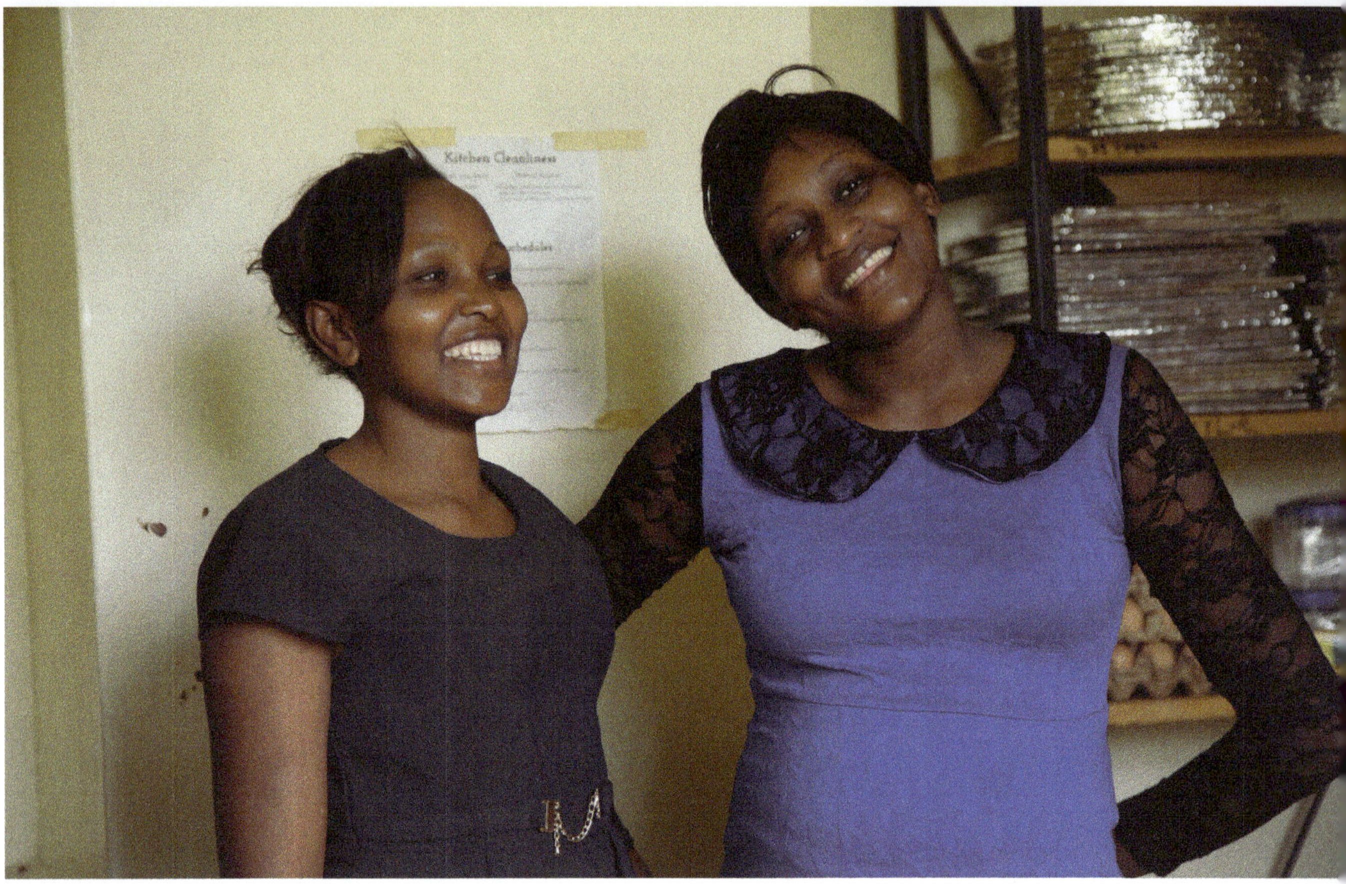
Kitchen Cleanliness

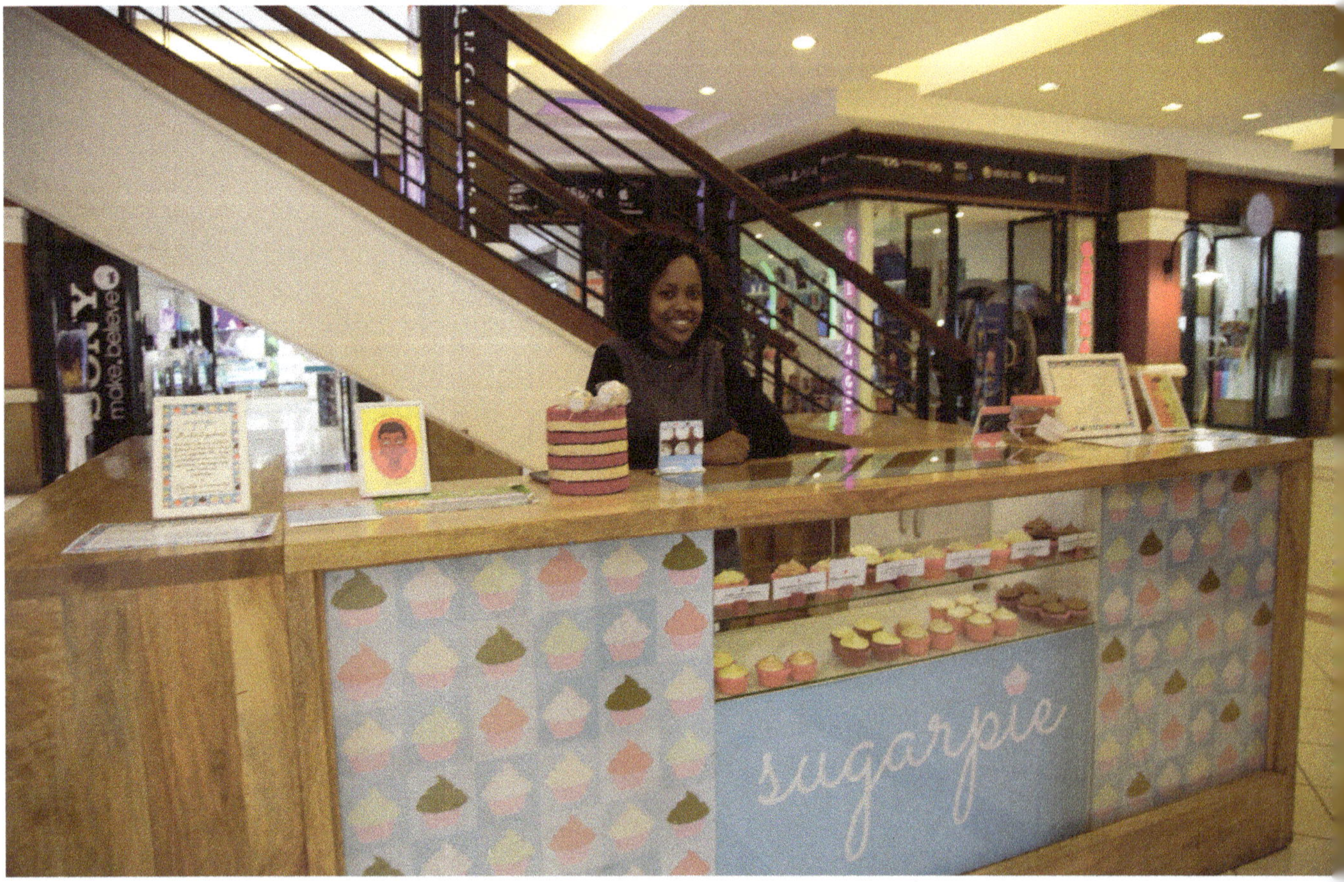
make.believe
sugarpie

Sugarpie

I started Sugarpie in the fall of 2013 in the hopes of creating delicious, all-natural desserts and good jobs. I was inspired by my housekeeper, Benedetta, who I'd met a year and a half before when I'd first moved to Nairobi. She used to go home and replicate the cakes that I'd bake at home on a coal-burning cookstove and I realized that opening a bakery would be a way to create a career path for individuals like her who were hard-working and ambitious, but didn't have much formal education. At the same time, I could fulfill my near-constant desire to eat yummy less-guilt dessert.

I moved to Nairobi nearly five years ago, after living in NYC for almost a year working on a tech startup and working as a line cook in a little West Village restaurant. This was after graduating from UPenn and spending a couple of months traveling and applying to and turning down grad school. One of my best friends from college was living here and she loved it, so I decided to come and check it out. I had a round-trip ticket, but I assumed that I'd stay, and of course, I did. After some dilly-dallying and about a year spent helping to launch a solar company start-up, I started Sugarpie.

After starting in my home and making deliveries, we eventually settled into a small office park and opened a shop at the Junction Mall in the Lavington neighborhood, in addition to our online ordering platform, one of the earliest in Nairobi. The bakery started out focusing exclusively on cupcakes, the idea was to create a something that was relatively small and affordable, to be accessible to wide audience. After about a year we started adding cakes and recently started doing cookies.

Most of the recipes are inspired by cakes that are universally loved, and others are creative interpretations of local flavors. I prioritized making everything completely natural, so without artificial colors, flavors or additives, which was pretty novel in Nairobi at the time, especially among bakeries. Most desserts were, and still are, loaded up with bright colors and artificial flavors, which while very affordable, didn't taste like much. I wanted to make cakes that tasted delicious first and foremost, and were also beautiful. As a result, we had to be creative with our recipes, adapting to not only the elevation, Nairobi is located at 5900 feet, but also the ingredients we could access. Since cupcakes generally require very few ingredients, it was important that each be really good quality. I found a supplier in Uganda that was producing fair-trade, organic vanilla for export to the UK, and managed to convince her to send some to us in Kenya, making Sugarpie her only Africa-based customer. Instead of using red food coloring, we substituted beetroot, which is readily available at most markets and started making jams out of local fruits, such as tree tomato, for frostings.

It's out of Sugarpie that the inspiration for this book came, and it's exciting to see not only how the business has grown, but how an ecosystem has developed and changed around us not just in restaurants, but food culture more generally in Nairobi.

~ MISONO ~

GRILLED SALMON WITH AVOCADO CREMA

 SERVES
4

Misono is fastidious about not overcooking their fish, which is particularly essential when you're working with a cut of high-quality salmon. The fillets should still have a spot of dark pink in the middle when you remove them from the pan. For an evenly cut piece of salmon, this takes about 4 minutes per side.

 TIME
Total Time: 45 minutes
Active Time: 45 minutes

 INGREDIENTS FOR THE SALMON
4 salmon fillets, 7 ounces (200 grams) each
½ cup (120 mL) sake (or dry sherry)
½ teaspoon salt
12 tablespoons butter

FOR THE AVOCADO CREMA
1 teaspoon neutral oil
1 small red onion, finely chopped
4-6 cloves garlic, minced
¼ cup (60 mL) sake
2 ripe avocados, pitted, peeled, and lightly mashed
2 teaspoons hot sauce (Misono uses Tabasco)
1 tablespoon butter
1 ½ cups (360 mL) heavy cream
2 tablespoons fish sauce
2 tablespoons light soy sauce
2 ounces (55 grams) drained anchovies (about 15 whole anchovies), finely chopped

TO SERVE
2 cups cooked rice (white, brown, or fried)
2 tablespoons olive oil
Sprinkle of salt
Small handful of chopped dill or parsley

 PREPARATION

1. Marinate the salmon: Place the salmon filets in a medium bowl. Sprinkle each with a little salt on both sides. Pour the sake over and let the salmon marinate for at least 30 minutes, or for up to 8 hours in the fridge.

2. Make the avocado crema: In a small saucepan, heat the oil over medium heat. Add the onion and garlic and cook until the garlic just starts to brown, 3-4 minutes. Reduce the heat to low and add the sake. Stir until most of the moisture has evaporated, then add the mashed avocado and the hot sauce. Stir over heat for 2-3 minutes, then take the pan off the heat and add the butter, cream, fish sauce, soy sauce, and chopped anchovies.

3. Blend the crema: Let the sauce cool for 5-10 minutes, then blend it in a blender or food processor. Taste; add additional fish sauce or soy sauce to bring it to your preferred saltiness.

4. Cook the salmon: Heat the butter in a large pan over high heat. Strain the salmon out of its marinade, then place the fillets, skin side down, and cook for about 4 minutes, until the bottom sides are golden brown. Flip and cook 4-6 minutes more, until the salmon is done to your liking. Let the fillets rest at least 5 minutes before serving.

5. Serve: Plate each salmon fillet over a mound of rice; drizzle the rice with a little olive oil and sprinkle it lightly with salt. Spoon the avocado crema on top or alongside. Sprinkle fresh herbs over.

NOTES

1. You don't have to blend the avocado sauce; whether you do or don't is mainly an aesthetic question. If you like the look of the sauce in the pan, serve it that way; blending it will make it both more homogenous and lighter in texture. If you have extra avocado sauce, store it in a tightly sealed container in the fridge for up to two days. It makes a great salad dressing, sandwich spread, or accompaniment to grilled vegetables.

2. If possible, pick fillets that are an even thickness, rather than ones with a thick center and long, thin edges. This helps ensure that the fish is cooked evenly throughout, not overdone on the edges.

── SUSHI SOO ──

DYNAMITE FUTO MAKI ROLL

MAKES
6 rolls

TIME
Total Time: 45 minutes
Active Time: 45 minutes

INGREDIENTS

2 cups (400 grams) uncooked sushi rice

2 cups (480 mL) water

1/3 cup (80 mL) rice vinegar

2 tablespoons sugar

½ teaspoon salt

6 sheets of seaweed

1 pound (450 grams) tempura prawns (see page X)

1-2 cucumbers, peeled and cut into long strips

1 ripe avocado, cut into thin strips

About 12 pieces takuwan (see page 204), optional

¼ cup (56 grams) mayonnaise

1 tablespoon sriracha (more or less, depending on your preference)

Soy sauce, wasabi, and pickled ginger, to serve

PREPARATION

1. Prepare the rice: Rinse the rice in water three times: the water should run clear. Then, combine the rice and water in a medium saucepan, bring to a boil, and simmer until the water is absorbed and the rice is tender, about 10 minutes.

2. In a small saucepan, combine the rice vinegar, sugar, and salt. Simmer until the sugar and salt dissolve.

3. Transfer the cooked rice into a glass mixing bowl. Pour the vinegar mixture over and stir to coat well. Let the rice cool completely.

4. Make the spicy mayo: In a small bowl, stir together the mayonnaise and the sriracha. Taste; add more sriracha to your liking.

5. Construct: Lay a rectangular piece of seaweed on a sushi rolling mat or a slightly damp kitchen towel. Cover the seaweed with a layer of rice, leaving one inch of seaweed uncovered at the top. Dab a little chili mayonnaise down the center of the rectangle, then place prawns, cucumber, avocado, and takuwan down the middle. Roll the seaweed up, using your hands to keep it pressed closed. When you get to the top, brush the border of seaweed at the top with a little water to help it adhere.

6. Cut: Use a very sharp knife to cut your roll into slices.

7. Serve: Serve with soy sauce, wasabi, and pickled ginger.

TAKUWAN (PICKLED DAIKON RADISH)

MAKES

about 1 pound pickled radish

TIME

Total Time: 3-4 days
Active Time: 10 minutes

INGREDIENTS

1 pound (450 grams) daikon radish, peeled and cut into long, thin strips

1 cup (240 mL) white vinegar

1 cup (240 mL) water

2 tablespoons salt

½ cup (100 grams) sugar

1 whole chili pepper, thinly sliced

PREPARATION

1. **Prepare the daikon:** Place the sliced daikon into wide-mouthed glass jars.

2. **Make the pickling liquid:** In a medium saucepan, heat the vinegar, water, salt, and sugar, stirring until the salt and sugar dissolve. Turn off the heat and add the chili pepper. Ladle this liquid over the daikon pieces; the liquid should fully cover them. Seal tightly and let the jars cool to room temperature.

3. **Pickle:** Refrigerate for 3-4 days, then use in sushi or as a post-meal digestion aid.

Cheka

Yuki and Kyohei met in high school where they used to dream about one day opening a restaurant together. Throughout high school and college they worked in restaurants -Yuki in a sushi restaurant and Kyohei in an izakaya - and they bonded over their love of food. After university, they each went their own ways, but never let go of their childhood dream.

Yuki fell in love with Zambia first. He lived in a village called Samfya, where he'd been sent by the Japanese government to be a volunteer teacher. Having been a star baseball player and majored in physical education in university, his job was to teach sports in the village school. For four years, he lived in a village that didn't have electricity or running water and taught physical education. He learned both English and the local language and fell so in love with the village that he stayed an extra six months after his posting. He tried to find a way to stay even longer, but unsuccessful, he returned to Japan. Trying to plot a way to get back to Africa, he pitched himself to a car export company in Japan to open an office for them in Mombasa.

Yuki moved to Mombasa and for five years worked in the car import business. He knew that he wanted to get into the restaurant business, though, and took advantage of his time on the coast to befriend fishermen and teach them how to fish in the Japanese way.

Meanwhile, Kyohei, who'd majored in Vietnamese in college, moved to Vietnam to work in an izakaya, and then New Zealand to work for a shipping company.
By 2013 they were ready to open their restaurant, and Yuki was convinced that Nairobi was the right place. There weren't any Japanese-owned Japanese restaurants, and all the Japanese restaurants focused on sushi. Given their love for izakaya-style food, it was obvious that their restaurant would be an izakaya, serving fried, salty, delicious small plates meant to be eaten while drinking.

Kyohei quit his job in July of 2014 and joined Yuki in Nairobi. They convinced five of their friends to come from Japan to help them build the furniture for the restaurant. Using scavenged wood, they built triangle-shaped tables for the outside patio and a loft indoors that overlooks the entire space. In 2014, on Valentine's Day, Cheka opened.

Given their backgrounds in shipping, they bring in containers regularly with ingredients from Japan. They have a full-time fisherman based in Mombasa who fishes for the restaurant and overnights the catch multiple times a week to the restaurant. They started a restaurant farm outside the city to grow traditional Japanese vegetables and herbs that they haven't been able to buy locally.

In early 2016, Kyohei left the partnership to start his own business making and selling to-go sushi in supermarkets. While still close friends, Yuki is now the sole proprietor, a permanent fixture in the restaurant. Yuki's goal for the restaurant was always to make good food, but also to create employment. His work in Zambia convinced him of the importance of job and opportunity creation, and he felt that he could make a difference by opening a restaurant. He bought a van specifically to take his employees home safely every night and has created an in-restaurant training program.

Walking into Cheka is a joyful experience. You're greeted by

Yuki, the bar staff, and smells of delicious food. When you sit down a waiter brings you a warm, minty towel, and then sets the table. All of the food is plated beautifully on traditional Japanese ceramics, and every detail is considered, from the delicate egg tamago to the perfectly juicy kaarage (fried chicken).

Cheka is on the forefront of the global ramen and izakaya trend, making authentic food that would be novel even in the most cosmopolitan of food cities. Nairobi is lucky to have Cheka.

s̄

~~ JARDIN DU PARIS ~~

SEAFOOD MARMITE

 SERVES
6

This may be the most decadent recipe of the bunch. If you need to reduce the price tag on this dish, you can opt to sub 9 ounces (250 grams) of potatoes, carrots, or cauliflower florets in for any of the seafood ingredients. We recommend keeping the mussels and prawns no matter what, but feel free to mix and match.

 TIME
Total Time: 30 minutes
Active Time: 30 minutes

 INGREDIENTS
18 ounces (500 grams) mussels, in the shell
10 ounces (300 grams) firm-fleshed fish
10 ounces (300 grams) lobster tail
10 ounces (300 grams) crab claw meat
10 ounces (300 grams) giant prawns, peeled medallions, shell removed
2 tablespoons butter
3 small yellow onions, chopped
8 cloves of garlic, minced
1 1/2 tablespoons minced ginger
1 teaspoon salt
3 cups (720 mL) dry white wine
3 tablespoons corn flour
2 cups (450 mL) heavy cream
Salt and pepper, to taste
1 bunch fresh parsley (about 1/2 cup / 25 grams), finely chopped
Steamed rice, to serve (optional)

 PREPARATION

1. **Prepare the seafood:** Check over the mussels to make sure all the shells are intact. Rinse twice in water to remove grit from the outsides of the shells. Cut the fish filet into large pieces. Chop the lobster tail and crab claws into large chunks. De-vein the prawns (if they aren't already).

2. **Sauté the vegetables:** In a large pot, melt the butter. Add the onions, garlic, ginger, and salt and cook for 2-3 minutes, just until the onions are looking shiny.

3. **Brown the seafood:** Add the lobster, crab, fish, and prawns and cook for about 3 minutes, just until you see the prawns begin to turn pink. Then, add the mussels.

4. **Simmer:** Pour the white wine over the mussels. (It won't be enough to cover everything in your pot; that's okay.) Immediately put a lid on the pot and cook for 5-7 minutes, until the wine comes to a rolling boil. Remove the lid; most of the mussels should be open by this point. Reduce the heat to medium-low and let the stew simmer, uncovered, for 10 minutes.

5. While the stew is simmering, stir the corn flour into the heavy cream in a medium bowl.

6. **Finish:** Add the heavy cream and bring the stew back to a simmer, stirring constantly. Taste and add salt and pepper as needed.

7. **Serve:** Garnish with chopped parsley and black pepper. Serve over rice (as Jardin du Paris did) or eat the stew on its own or with toasted bread.

208 | FISH & SEAFOOD MAINS

~ BODYZONE ~

SAMAKI MOSHI

 **SERVES**
6

Quite literally meaning "smoke fish" in Swahili, this dish is traditionally cooked in a charcoal oven, producing fish that is part grilled, part smoked. As with the poisson sauce (page 212), you can opt to cook an entire fish instead of fillets, if you wish; it shouldn't take much longer to cook than the fillets, but make a small cut into the fattest part of the fish to make sure it's cooked through before serving.

 TIME
Total Time: 20 minutes
Active Time: 20 minutes

 SPECIAL TOOLS
Outdoor grill (gas or wood-burning), with a lid

 INGREDIENTS
2 cups hardwood chips (hickory, oak, cherry)
6 6-ounce (170-gram) Nile Perch or tilapia fillets, with the skin
4-6 tablespoons olive oil
2 teaspoons salt
1 tomato, sliced, to garnish
1 onion, cut into thin rings, to garnish

PREPARATION

1. Prepare the smoking wood: Soak the wood chips in water for about one hour. Then, place the chips in a heat-safe container (like a tin-foil pan) and cover with tin foil. Poke several holes in the tin foil so that smoke can escape.

2. Prepate the grill: Place the container of wood chops on the grill, close the lid, and put the grill's heat to high.

3. Prepare the fish: While the grill is heating, rub the fillets all over with oil, then sprinkle with salt. Check to see that the grill has begun to fill with smoke, then place the fillets on the grill, skin side up, and close the lid. Grill 10-15 minutes, until the fillets are cooked through.

4. Serve: Serve the fish with sliced tomato and onion and a side of rice and fried plantains (see page 196).

BODYZONE

SAUCE POISSON
(NILE PERCH WITH RED PEPPER SAUCE)

SERVES
6

At Bodyzone, they serve whole fish, complete with the head, fins, and tail. If you have access to whole fish and don't mind dealing with bones, then do it as they do. For a simpler eating experience, buy boneless fish filets, with or without the skin. The cooking time remains the same for the whole fish and the filets.

TIME
Total Time: 40 minutes
Active Time: 20 minutes

INGREDIENTS

6 6-ounce (170-gram) boneless Nile Perch fillets

5 cloves garlic, peeled and roughly chopped

3 sweet red peppers, seeded and roughly chopped

3 yellow onions, peeled and roughly chopped

4 tablespoons tomato paste

2 teaspoons salt, plus more for the fillets

Pinch of pepper

PREPARATION

1. **Preheat** the oven to 375F (190C).

2. **Make the sauce:** Place the garlic, sweet peppers, onions, tomato paste, salt, and pepper in the bowl of a food processor. Process until you have a fairly smooth sauce, about 1 minute in total. Taste; add salt to your liking. Set the sauce aside.

3. **Bake the fish:** Place each fish fillet atop a large rectangle of aluminum foil. Sprinkle each fillet with a bit of salt, then spoon a generous amount of the red pepper sauce over. Fold the tin foil to completely cover the fish, place the foil packets on a baking tray, and bake for 20 minutes. After 20 minutes, unfold the foil packets and bake for 5 minutes more to allow a bit of the extra moisture to evaporate. Make a small cut into the center of one fillet; if it's white to the center, the fish is ready.

4. **Serve:** Serve the fish with a side of rice and fried plantains (page 196).

~ TRATTORIA ~

CRAB & GINGER PASTA

 SERVES
2-3

This dish is not traditional; Gaetano was inspired by local ingredients when he created it. With a little bit of fusion flair, this pasta dish has evolved into something truly unique and bursts with character and flavour. This simple recipe requires few ingredients but relies on premium fresh crabs.

 TIME
Total Time: 45 minutes
Active Time: 45 minutes

 SPECIAL TOOLS
Nutcracker or small mallet

 INGREDIENTS
1 lemon, halved
1 celery stalk, halved
1 carrot, halved
2 medium live crabs (or 7 ounces / 200 grams lump crab meat)
Bowl of ice
9 ounces (250 grams) dry spaghetti pasta
2 tablespoons olive oil
1 tablespoon thinly sliced ginger
6 green onions, chopped
2 green chillies, seeded and minced
½ teaspoon sugar
2 cloves of garlic, thinly sliced
¼ cup (60 mL) white wine
¾ cup (180 mL) chicken stock
2 tablespoons light soy sauce
Salt, to taste
Extra handful of green onions, to garnish

 PREPARATION

1. Poach the crabs: Bring a pot of lightly salted water to a boil. Add the lemon, celery and carrot and boil for 5-10 minutes. Then, grasp your crabs from the behind and plunge them into the water. Boil for 15 minutes.

2. Prepare the crab meat: Remove the crabs from the pot and plunge them into a bowl of ice. Once completely cool, set the first crab on a cutting board. Remove the top shell, then flip the crab over and remove the triangular piece of shell on the underside. Rinse the crabs, cleaning away the gills on each side. Remove the legs and claws; use a nutcracker to crack the shell and remove the meat. Crack the body in half by hand and remove the meat. Place all the cleaned meat in a bowl, then repeat with the second crab.

3. Boil the pasta: Discard the crab cooking liquid, rinse out the pan, and refill it with enough lightly salted water to cook your pasta. Boil according to the package instructions for al dente, then rinse the pasta in cold water and set it aside.

4. While the pasta is cooking, **make the sauce:** Heat a large pan over medium high heat and add the olive oil. Add the ginger, green onion and chili and cook for 3-4 minutes. Then, add the sugar, garlic, and crab meat and cook for 2 minutes more. Deglaze the pan with white wine, then add the chicken stock, soy sauce, and a pinch of salt. Simmer for 3-5 minutes.

5. Assemble: Add the cooked pasta directly into the sauce and cook for 1-2 minutes, just until the pasta is warmed and has absorbed some of the sauce. Taste; add salt to your liking.

6. Garnish: Sprinkle extra green onions over the pasta and serve with a sprinkle of black pepper.

NOTES

If the idea of plunging conscious crabs into boiling water bothers you, you can place the live crabs in a large container and then put the container in the freezer for 15-20 minutes. This numbs the crabs, making them both less sensitive to heat and less likely to try and pinch you.

Juniper Social

Juniper Social introduced Nairobi to Mason jar cocktails, rustic pallet furniture, and Pinterest-worthy interiors. To say that it completely changed the nightlife scene would be an understatement. It makes sense that the person to introduce this aesthetic would be young and trendy, and indisputably, this bar and restaurant is a true reflection of the vision of its founder, Rhi Pulford.

Rhi moved to Nairobi to work for an agricultural social enterprise, but quit after three months to pursue her passion for gin and food. She started out by hosting backyard brunches at her house, partly to make some cash, partly to indulge her love for hosting, and partly as market research. The brunches would regularly sell out, as fellow young expats and hip Kenyans packed her sprawling garden. Eventually her five housemates tired of sharing their house with a restaurant, and Rhi set her sights on creating something bigger and more permanent.

Coming from Australia, she envisioned bringing the simple, relaxed and rustic bar culture from home to Nairobi. She wanted to create a place where you could get great cocktails and have a conversation. She looked at over thirty locations before settling on the current one, which is located near the bustling bar district of Westlands. It's set on a large property with towering trees and an expansive garden. Working on a tight budget, she converted the dilapidated house into a pub, designing much of the furniture herself and using recycled materials where possible. She called her style "ad-hoc vintage." Looking around at the hay-covered ground, stacked crates topped with brightly coloring cushions, and wine bottles vases hanging along the walls, it seems like an accurate description. Juniper opened in January of 2014, and quickly became the place to go for ice cold cocktails. Their signature drinks are made with gin, Rhi's favorite liquor, and many are twists on classic cocktails incorporating local flavors.

As a vegetarian who eats fish, Rhi designed a menu that is vegetable-forward, focusing on salads and vegetarian-friendly options. Inspired by the multiculturalism of Australian cuisine, many of the items incorporate Asian flavors.

Juniper Social represents a new wave of immigrant-run bars and restaurants that target a younger clientele who want good drinks and food, but also an ambiance that feels trendy and cool. Furthermore, Rhi is one of a wave of young expat entrepreneurs who have made their way to Nairobi in recent years inspired by the idea of social entrepreneurship – creating social impact through market-based organizations. She made the transition from working for one to starting her own, which in many ways reflects a larger trend globally of young people breaking out of corporate culture to become entrepreneurs. Unlike previous waves of immigrants to Nairobi who came by accident seeking work or adventure, this newer wave has come with a clear intention of somehow changing the world, and they're finding different and creative ways of doing it.

NOTE Juniper Social closed in August 2016.

Desserts

220	GALETTE DES ROIS	Belle Ambiance
222	BLACK CAKE	Taste of Jamaica
223	BURNT SUGAR	Taste of Jamaica
226	CREME CARAMEL	Fogo Gaucho
228	VANILLA CHAI CAKE	Sugarpie
230	APPLE CRISP	Moniko's
234	CHOCOLATE MARSHMALLOW SAMOSAS	Purdy Arms
236	MATCHA GREEN TEA CAKE	Sushi Soo

─── BELLE AMBIANCE ───

GALETTE DES ROIS

SERVES
8

The history of the galette des rois (king cake) is long and studded with intrigue, including a 16th-century standoff between France's boulangeries (where breads & cakes were sold) and pâtisseries (where one finds pastries)—but the important thing to know is that this classic dish is fully within reach of the home cook. If you'd like to celebrate three kings' day in the traditional way, hide a whole almond, uncooked bean, or small porcelain figurine inside the galette. Whoever finds it gets to be king for the day.

TIME
Total Time: 7 hours, or up to 26 hours
Active Time: 45 minutes

INGREDIENTS
¼ cup (40 grams) raisins
2 tablespoons white or golden rum
¾ cup (175 grams) peeled, slivered almonds (or almond flour)
7 tablespoons (105 grams) butter
½ cup (100 grams) sugar
¼ teaspoon almond extract (optional)
¼ teaspoon salt
1 package puff pastry (around 14 ounces/400 grams)
1 egg

PREPARATION

1. **Soak the raisins:** In a small bowl, combine the raisins and the rum. Let the raisins soak for at least 30 minutes.

2. **Make the filling:** Place the almonds in the bowl of a food processor. Blend until they are thoroughly powdered. Add the butter and sugar and blend until the mixture is homogenous. Stir in the almond extract and salt.

3. **Chill the filling:** Stir the soaked raisins into the almond mixture. Chill the almond filling in a covered bowl in the fridge for at least 4 hours, or overnight.

4. **Prepare the dough:** Roll the puff pastry out into a large rectangle about 20" (50 centimeters) wide and 10" (25 centimeters) tall. Find a large dinner plate or mixing bowl with roughly a 10" (25 centimeter) diameter. Use the rim of the plate to make an outline of a circle on one half of the dough, then make another circular outline on the other half. Use a sharp knife or a pizza roller to cut out the two circles. Roll up the scraps and set them aside for another use. Place one of the circles on a lightly greased baking sheet.

5. **Preheat** the oven to 350F (175C).

6. **Build the galette:** Remove the filling from the fridge. Spread the filling onto the circle of pastry that you've placed on the baking sheet, leaving about an inch of border. Gently beat the egg in a small dish and use a pastry brush or spoon to spread the egg around the border. Place the second circle of pastry atop the first, pressing the edges down where you've applied the egg wash. Fold the bottom layer of pastry over the top one and crimp the edges as you would for a pie. Brush the top of the galette with the remaining egg wash and lightly score the pastry with a sharp paring knife.

7. **Bake:** Bake the galette in the middle of your oven for 20 minutes, or until it is nicely browned on top & bottom. If the top browns before the rest of the pastry is cooked, tent it with tin foil.

8. **Cool:** This galette is best served at room temperature. Allow it to cool for at least 2 hours, then slice and serve.

~ TASTE OF JAMAICA ~

BLACK CAKE

 SERVES
8+

This is the booziest cake we've ever made. It truly does get better with time, so if you have the will power to let it sit for one or even two days, your patience will be rewarded.

 TIME
Total Time: 3 days – 1 week
Active Time: 20 minutes

 INGREDIENTS

2 cups (about 360 grams) mixed dried fruit (raisins, apricots, cranberries, cherries)
1 cup (240 mL) Guinness stout
¼ cup (60 mL) brandy
½ to ¾ cup (120-180 mL) rum, divided
¾ cup (170 grams) butter
½ cup (100 grams) granulated sugar
3 medium eggs
1 teaspoon vanilla extract
¼ teaspoon freshly grated nutmeg
3 tablespoons burnt sugar (see opposite page)
1 cup (130 grams) flour
2 teaspoons baking powder
Vanilla ice cream, to serve
Freshly ground nutmeg, to garnish

 PREPARATION

1. Soak the fruit: Place the dried fruit in a large jar with a lid. Cover with the Guinness, brandy, and 1/4 cup of the rum. If the liquid doesn't completely cover the dried fruit, add more rum to cover. Seal and refrigerate for at least 3 days, or for up to 2 weeks.

2. Preheat the oven to 350F (175C).

3. Blend the fruit: Place the soaked dried fruit, along with any extra liquid in the jar, in a blender. Blend for about 30 seconds, until the mixture is well puréed.

4. Make the batter: In a large bowl, cream together the butter and sugar. Add the eggs one by one, beating well after each addition. Add the vanilla, nutmeg, and burnt sugar. Add the flour and baking powder and stir gently to combine, then fold in the puréed fruits.

5. Bake: Pour the batter into a lightly greased 9" square cake pan, bundt pan, or bread pan. Bake for 35 - 45 minutes, checking every 15 minutes to ensure the top isn't browning too quickly; tent with tin foil if it is. The cake is ready when a fork inserted into the middle comes out clean.

6. Splash with rum: While the cake is still warm, poke it all over with a toothpick. Pour 1/4 cup (60 mL) rum over; for a particularly boozy cake, add another 1/4 cup. Let the cake sit for at least one hour, or ideally overnight, before eating. It will be very moist and quite strong.

7. Serve: Once the cake has had time to soak up the rum, cut it into squares and serve with a scoop of vanilla ice cream and a sprinkle of nutmeg.

~ TASTE OF JAMAICA ~

BURNT SUGAR

YIELD
1/2 cup

Despite the somewhat off-putting name, this variation on simple syrup is a fantastic addition to almost any baked good. It's a must in black cake, but it also adds nice caramelized flavor to virtually any cake, cookie, or sweet bread.

TIME
Total Time: 3 days – 1 week
Active Time: 20 minutes

PREPARATION

1. Make the burnt sugar: In a small saucepan, melt the granulated sugar. Resist the urge to stir; you can swirl the pan occasionally, but otherwise let the sugar melt on its own. When the sugar is dark amber in color, take it off the heat and add the boiling water, being careful as the sugar may spatter a bit. Whisk until the mixture is smooth, then let it cool to room temperature.

2. Store: Burnt sugar keeps well in a sealed jar in the pantry.

INGREDIENTS
¼ cup (50 grams) granulated sugar
¼ cup (60 mL) boiling water

Han Di Yuan

Life in Nairobi is a constant exploration in identity, ethnicity, and culture. Han Di Yuan is a perfect example of this dynamic. The restaurant first opened with a big sign that declared its name to be Korean Barbeque. A few months later, the "Korean" part was covered, so the name became Barbeque. Now, it's back to Korean Barbeque, with Chinese characters below. So what kind of restaurant is it? Well, it's Chinese-owned Korean barbeque with Chinese ingredients and flavors. How is that possible? China does share a border with Korea and, as culture and cuisine are permeable, Chinese Korean barbeque is a cuisine all its own.

A meal at Han Di Yuan starts with a server bringing out a metal box of coals that fits into a cut-out square in the center of the table. Next comes a small dish with various spice mixes for dipping. One is predominantly cumin and fennel, and the other tastes strongly of toasted chilis and black sesame. Then a small bowl of soy sauce comes, along with toasted rice tea. And finally, the star of the show: plates and plates of meat. There's pork belly marinated in kimchi, beef ribs marinated in soy, dried fish and squid, and little steamed bun toasts. For starch, you can get kimchi fried rice or a bowl of spicy beef noodles. Or, you can skip the meat all together and go for their version of hot pot, which is basically a massive steaming bowl of spicy beef stock with all sorts of veggies and meats. So is it Korean Chinese or Chinese Korean? Hard to say, but definitely both.

Growing up, Xiao Yi moved a lot with his family, leaving home at sixteen to look for work. He moved to Nairobi six years ago to work as a barber. He opened a small shop in the China Center, a large shopping center with a variety of stores and restaurants (not all Chinese), where he cut hair for five years. In January 2015, he decided to open a restaurant serving the food of his home, Dong Bei, a medium-sized city in the far north of China located on the Korean border.

At the restaurant, he serves what he describes as home-style food. This is the food he grew up eating, and he tries to keep it as close to what he remembers as possible. About 80% of the ingredients he uses are imported, including sauces and spices. Since barbeque is all about the meat, he spent six months looking for a supplier until he found one that was willing to learn the cuts he needed and age the meat to his liking. He uses traditional Chinese greens in his dishes, and he hasn't had any problems sourcing fresh vegetables from local farms.

Han Di Yuan exemplifies the idea that food is borderless. The spice mixes are distinctly Western Chinese, or Uighur, where the food is deeply influenced by its proximity to Central Asia and the Middle East. Kimchi, usually thought of as the hallmark of Korean food, is common in the Dong Bei region of China. And barbeque? Well, pretty much every food culture in the world has some form of meat cooked directly over fire. And now that all of this is being cooked and eaten in Nairobi, it's becoming part of African cuisine.

~ FOGO GAUCHO ~

CREME CARAMEL

SERVES
8

This recipe has a short list of simple ingredients, but the procedure requires some patience and attention. Be sure to keep an eye on your sugar as it caramelizes: you want it to have a rich amber color, but not much darker than that.

TIME
Total Time: 7 hours or more
Active Time: 30 minutes

INGREDIENTS FOR THE CARAMEL
⅔ cup (135 grams) granulated sugar
⅓ cup (80 mL) water

FOR THE CUSTARD
4 eggs
1 cup (280 mL) sweetened condensed milk
2 cups (480 mL) full-fat milk
Nob of butter, to grease the pan

PREPARATION

1. Preheat the oven: Heat your oven to 350F (175C). Place an 8-inch pie dish in the oven to warm (this will help keep the caramel from seizing when poured into the dish).

2. Make the caramel: Combine the sugar and the water in a large, shallow saucepan. Turn on the heat and whisk just until the sugar dissolves; then, stop whisking and allow the sugar to caramelize. You may gently swirl the pan to distribute the heat, but resist the urge to stir.

3. Prepare the custard: While the sugar is cooking, which will take 8-10 minutes, combine the eggs, sweetened condensed milk, and milk in a large bowl. Whisk briskly for 3 minutes, until the mixture is light yellow in color.

4. Grease the pan: Remove the warm pie dish from the oven and grease it with butter.

5. Construct:
When the sugar has turned a deep amber color, remove it from heat and pour it immediately into the pie dish. Angle the dish to spread the sugar around the entire bottom. Do this quickly, before the sugar can harden. Allow the sugar to cool for 3-4 minutes. Place the pie dish into another filled with about 1/2 inch of warm water, then pour the egg mixture into the pie dish.

6. Bake: Bake the custard in its water bath 45 minutes to one hour, checking it every 20 minutes. The crème caramel is done when the middle no longer jiggles when you gently shake the pan. If the surface begins to brown, tent it lightly with tin foil.

7. Cool: Once out of the oven, allow the crème caramel to cool for at least six hours, or ideally overnight in the fridge.

8. To serve:
Gently loosen the sides of the custard with a butter knife, cover the pie dish with a large plate or cutting board, and invert: you'll have a layer of glassy caramel on the top. Cut into slices and serve.

~~~ SUGARPIE ~~~

VANILLA CHAI CAKE

 SERVES
8-12

This cake is a perfect celebration or everyday dessert. It's simple enough that kids love it, and complex enough that adults crave it.

 TIME
Total Time: 45 minutes
Active Time: 15 minutes

 INGREDIENTS FOR THE CAKE

2 eggs
1 cup (245 grams) plain yogurt
½ cup (120 grams) vegetable oil
½ teaspoon vanilla extract
1 cup (100 grams) granulated sugar
2 cups (260 grams) sifted all-purpose flour
½ teaspoon baking soda
1 ½ teaspoon baking powder
¼ teaspoon salt
½ teaspoon chai spice mix

FOR THE FROSTING

½ cup (114 grams) unsalted butter, softened
1 ½ cup (190 grams) icing sugar, sifted
1 teaspoon vanilla extract
2 tablespoons milk
½ teaspoon chai spice mix

FOR THE CHAI SPICE MIX

½ teaspoon ground cardamom
¼ teaspoon ground cinnamon
⅛ teaspoon ground nutmeg
⅛ teaspoon ground cloves

 PREPARATION

1. **Preheat** oven to 350F (175C).
2. **Prepare your pans:** Butter and flour two 8-inch round pans.
3. **Make the cake batter:** In a medium bowl, stir together the eggs, yogurt, oil, vanilla and sugar in a large bowl. In another bowl, sift together the flour, baking soda, baking powder, chai spice mix, and salt. Gently mix the dry ingredients into the wet ingredients until incorporated. Pout the batter into the prepared pans.
4. **Bake:** Bake for about 30 minutes, or until a fork inserted in the middle comes out clean.
5. While the cakes are baking, **make the frosting:** In a medium bowl, cream the butter until light and fluffy. Slowly add the icing sugar, making sure that it's fully incorporated. Add the vanilla, milk, and chai spice mix. Beat for 1-2 minutes.
6. **Frost the cakes:** Once the cakes are completely cooled, frost them with a rubber spatula.
7. **Serve:** Cut the cakes into wedges, sprinkle with extra chai spice mix, and serve.

~~~ MONIKO'S ~~~

APPLE CRUMBLE

 **SERVES**
6-8

This recipe is simple, very quick to throw together, and almost universally beloved. When choosing your apples, get a mix of tart varieties (like Granny Smith) and sweeter ones (like Pink Lady).

 TIME
Total Time: 1 hour 15 minutes
Active Time: 15 minutes

 INGREDIENTS
1 ¼ cup (160 grams) white flour
1 ⅔ cups (150 grams) oats
½ cup (100 grams) white sugar
½ cup (105 grams) packed brown sugar
½ teaspoon salt
⅔ cup (150 grams) melted butter
7-10 apples (1 ½ pounds / 700 grams), cored and cut into wedges
Vanilla ice cream, to serve

 PREPARATION

1. Preheat the oven to 350F (175C).

2. Make the topping: In a large bowl, combine the flour, oats, sugar, brown sugar, and salt. Add the melted butter and stir until you have even crumbs.

3. Bake: Grease a 9-inch square baking dish with butter. Place the sliced apples in the dish and cover them completely with the topping. Bake until the apples are fork-tender and the topping is golden brown, about 45 minutes. (If the topping begins to brown before the apples are cooked, tent with tin foil.)

4. Serve: Let the crumble cool for at least 15 minutes. Serve warm with a generous scoop of vanilla ice cream.

Chengdu Impressions

Everyone dreams at some point of having an opportunity to wipe the slate clean and start over. Whether it's in a professional context of wishing to try a different career, or personal of moving far away and becoming someone new, for different motivations and desires, most of us have thought about it. Ellen Bie actually did it.

Having lived and worked in Chengdu her entire life, Nairobi represented a true escape for Ellen, a clean break from the past. She'd spent over a decade running her own restaurants in Chengdu with her husband and family, but following a divorce, she decided she wanted to get away and try doing something on her own. She'd visited Nairobi three times at the recommendation of a college friend who was living here, each time exploring the idea of making a permanent move. When she finally decided to make the move, her friend helped her to find the location for the restaurant and settle into life in Nairobi. She knew that she wanted to open a restaurant here because of her extensive experience in the industry, and also because she believed hers would be the only authentically Sichuanese restaurant in the city.

Often when people talk about Chinese food, it's in reference to the type of Chinese food found in most American cities, an amalgam of Chinese and American tastes that is in many ways a cuisine of its own. Ask a Chinese person, though, and you'll be given a lesson on the regional cuisines of China, of which there are eight main groups. Sichuan is one of them, often characterized by numbing spices and bold flavors. Chengdu, the provincial capital of Sichuan, is arguably its culinary capital. Designated by UNESCO as a "Capital of Gastronomy," the city is home to endless good eating.

Recognizing her unique position as an expert in the cuisine of Chengdu, Ellen opened Chengdu Impressions with the hope of serving traditional cuisine authentic to her tastes. Walking into the restaurant, you're welcomed into an entryway decorated in the style of a Chengdu tea ceremony. A zither sits off to the corner and in the center is a table laid out with a complete tea set. Continue walking and you start to smell that sweet, sour and spicy signature of Sichuan food. All of the tables are set-up for hotpot, invented in Chongqing, another Sichuan culinary destination, but their dishes are equally as exciting.

Within months of opening, Ellen's brother joined her as a partner in the restaurant. He was a chef in their restaurants in Chengdu, and worked briefly in the US so that his son could go to school there. Perhaps it's a cliché, but being the child of Chinese immigrants myself, for many immigrants from China, the ultimate goal is to provide a good education for their children. This is what truly motivates both Ellen and her brother, who have traveled far and wide in the hopes of making enough money to send their children to school in the US. Ellen left behind her teenage daughter in China so that she could try to earn more money in Nairobi. She's dedicated her life here to working constantly, so that in five years when her daughter is applying for college, she can go to the US.

It's part of every immigrant's dream to make a better life, and Ellen is dogged in her pursuit. She isn't just here to make a good life and see what happens, she is on a mission to prove herself.

 PURDY ARMS

CHOCOLATE MARSHMALLOW SAMOSAS

 SERVES
6-8

Think of this delectable dessert as The Purdy Arms' creative reinterpretation of a s'more.

 TIME
Total Time: 1 hour 30 minutes
Active Time: 30 minutes

INGREDIENTS

1 package samosa or wonton wrappers (or 20 2-inch x 8-inch sheets)
1 1/2 cups 225 grams) dark chocolate chips
1 cup (45 grams) mini marshmallows
1/4 cup (32 grams) all-purpose flour
4-6 tablespoons water
3 cups (720 mL) neutral oil, for frying
Vanilla ice cream, to serve

 PREPARATION

1. Make pastry glue: In a small bowl, whisk together the flour and the water. Set it aside.

2. Fold: Place a samosa wrapper on a clean work surface. In the palm of your hand, press together a tablespoon of marshmallows and a tablespoon of chocolate chips; it should form a loosely adhered ball. Place the chocolate chips and marshmallows at the top of the wrapper and fold the top-right corner of the samosa across the filling, so the top of the wrapper is in the shape of a right triangle. Fold the triangle directly downward, then continue the diagonal and downward folds until you come to the end of the wrapper. Brush a little of the pastry glue on the final flap of the wrapper to help it adhere. Place the folded samosa on a plate and continue folding until you run out of filling.

3. Freeze: Cover the samosas with plastic wrap and freeze for at least one hour. (This helps to keep the chocolate and marshmallow from leaking out when you fry the samosas.)

4. Fry: In a wide, deep pan, heat the oil over medium high heat. Carefully place one samosa in the oil; if it sizzles on contact, the oil is ready. Fry the samosas in batches for 3-4 minutes, until they are golden brown all over. Use a slotted spoon to remove them from the oil and place them on a paper towel-lined plate.

5. Serve: Eat the samosas with a generous scoop of vanilla ice cream.

NOTES

If you don't have mini marshmallows, just cut big ones. Scissors work better than a knife for this.

~~~ SUSHI SOO ~~~

MATCHA GREEN TEA CAKE

SERVES
6-8

Sushi Soo's bakery is filled with fresh-from-the-oven delicacies that combine classic French baking with Korean flavors. They present this green tea cake in two forms: a classic roll and individual cakes coated in a layer of cake crumbs.

TIME
Total Time: 1 hour
Active Time: 30 minutes

INGREDIENTS FOR THE CAKE

1 cup (130 grams) all-purpose flour
1 teaspoon baking powder
1/2 teaspoon salt
2 tablespoons matcha green tea powder
1/2 cup (114 grams) butter
1/2 cup plus 2 tablespoons (125 grams) granulated sugar
5 eggs
1/2 cup (120 grams) finely sliced almonds (optional)
1/2 cup (50 grams) cranberries (optional)

FOR THE FROSTING

1 cup (250 mL) cold heavy cream
2 tablespoons icing sugar

PREPARATION

1. Preheat the oven to 350F (175C). Line a large rectangular baking dish with parchment paper.

2. Make the batter: In a medium bowl, sift together the flour, baking powder, salt, and matcha green tea powder. Set the dry ingredients aside. In a large bowl, cream the butter and sugar until very smooth. Add the eggs one by one, beating well after each addition. Slowly fold in the dry ingredients. Fold in the almonds and cranberries, if using. Pour the batter into the prepared pan.

3. Bake: Bake for 8-12 minutes, until a toothpick inserted into the middle comes out clean.

4. While the cake is baking, make the frosting: Put the heavy cream into a large bowl. Whip the cream by hand or with a hand mixer until it begins to thicken. Slowly add the sugar and continue whipping until the cream is very thick.

5. Shape: Now is the time to decide whether to make a rolled cake or individual layer cakes. To make a roll:

  a. Pre-roll: Gently separate the cake from the parchment paper with a butter knife, then invert it onto another piece of baking parchment or a clean kitchen towel. While the cake is still warm, gently roll it up, starting from the short end. Allow the cake to cool to room temperature in this shape. (Rolling the cake while it's still warm keeps it from cracking later.)

  b. Frost & serve: Gently unroll the cake. Spread the whipped cream evenly all over its surface, then roll it back up. Cut into slices and serve with a sprinkle of icing sugar.

To make mini layer cakes:

  a. Cut: Once the cake has cooled to room temperature, use a cookie cutter or a jar to cut out circles in multiples of three. Place the cake scraps into a large bowl and crumble them finely with your hands.

  b. Build: Place a circle of cake on a clean work surface. Spread a thin layer of frosting over it. Repeat this twice more, finishing with three layers each of cake and frosting. Then, gently frost the outside of the cake; it doesn't have to be the prettiest frosting job. Place the layer cake in the bowl of crumbs and roll to cover it with crumbs on all sides. Continue with the remaining cake, frosting, and crumbs.

c. Serve: Serve the cakes individually with a dusting of icing sugar and extra matcha green tea powder, if desired.

NOTES

No green tea powder on hand? You can make this cake without the green tea, though it will lack its distinctive color and subtle taste of matcha. To add alternative flavor, consider adding 2 teaspoons vanilla, almond, or orange extract along with the eggs.

Marula Mercantile

Seth Johnson and Alyson Schultz were looking for an adventure. Seasoned chefs trained in some of America's most distinguished restaurants, they left behind Michelin-starred kitchens to explore Kenya and do something on their own. Their initial impetus for moving was that Alyson had been offered a consulting contract with one of Kenya's largest chains to help create a new, high-end pizza restaurant. They moved together and Seth joined the same company. After a year and a half, they decided it was time to venture off on their own.

Food culture in America over the last decade has moved increasingly towards organic, farm-oriented eating. Kenyan food culture in some ways has too, though paradoxically. Kenya has an agriculture-based economy where most people are farmers, or have a close connection to their agricultural past. But as the country develops, as is the trend globally, those with money are moving towards processed and fast food. While the majority of Kenyans eat a relatively healthy diet of legumes and vegetables, a growing middle and elite class are moving in the direction of mid-century America.

Seth and Alyson developed their style of cooking in some of America's most forward-looking restaurants, notably Chez Panisse, helmed by Alice Waters, pioneer of the local and organic food movement, and Eleven Madison Park, New York City's three Michelin starred temple to farmer-focused food. Given these backgrounds, it's no surprise that they opened a restaurant that prides itself on the sourcing of organic ingredients and making everything in-house.

Marula Mercantile opened in 2015 and quickly became known as a restaurant that made crave-able American classics, but fresher, lighter and healthier. With a love for both fine and casual dining, they serve refined comfort food, simply prepared with a focus on ingredients. Local ingredients in the American farmers-market jargon are not hard to find in Nairobi. The city is surrounded by rich farmland and produce often makes a short journey from farm to market to table. However, lack of regulation on pesticides and diversity of seed varietals means that groceries are often filled with just one type of each vegetable, and grown in unknown conditions.

As a result, Marula's efforts to support farms that use organic practices and encourage biodiversity are unique and novel. They source vegetables from an organic farm run by a young American-Kenyan couple, and occasionally provide them with seeds of plants they want to source but haven't been able to find. Upon request from Marula, this farm cuts the lettuces younger than is standard practice, resulting in salads of baby greens. They source pork from a small family farm in Navaisha, and use it for the house-cured bacon. They found a woman who lives just down the street from the restaurant who provides them with the "best eggs laid anywhere."

Marula, along with Juniper Social, represents a new wave of Nairobi establishments that are focused on great food and drinks, but also a new ethos around food. They're not just encouraging customers to think about what they eat, but how they eat.

s̄

Drinks

242	TRI-LEVEL JUICE	Abyssinia
243	THAI ICED TEA	Som Tam Thai
246	GUINESS PUNCH	Taste of Jamaica
247	CHUHAI (GRAPEFRUIT COCKTAIL)	Cheka
248	GIN DAWA	Juniper Social
250	GIN BASIL FIZZ	Juniper Social
256	BLOODY MARY	Marula Mercantile
257	CAPE FEAR PUNCH	Marula Mercantile

~~~ ETHIOPIAN ~~~

TRI-LEVEL JUICE

SERVES
3-4

These elaborate and beautiful juices are ubiquitous in Ethiopia. Although some combination of avocado, mango, and papaya is most common, you can also mix and match to your liking, subbing in pineapple or carrot juice for the mango or papaya.

TIME
Total Time: 10 minutes
Active Time: 10 minutes

INGREDIENTS
2 medium avocados
1-2 medium mangos
1-2 medium papaya
Juice of 2 limes
¼ cup (50 grams) sugar, plus more to taste
1 cup (240 mL) water, plus more as needed

PREPARATION

1. Prep the fruits: Peel, pit, and roughly chop the avocadoes, mangoes, and papaya.

2. Blend the avocado: Place the avocado in a blender. Add the lime juice, sugar, and water. Blend; when the mixture looks smooth, take a taste and add more lime juice or sugar to your liking. The mixture will be more smoothie-like than juice-like. Pour the blended avocado into 3-4 glasses, filling each one about 1/3 full.

3. Blend the mango and papaya: Blend the mango until it is very smooth. Pour the mango on top of the avocado. Blend the papaya and top off the glasses.

4. Serve: Squeeze a little extra lime juice over, then enjoy these juices as a healthy breakfast, afternoon refresher, or light dessert.

—— SOM TAM THAI ——

THAI ICED TEA

SERVES
4-6

Those familiar with Kenya will recognize the spices that are added to this brew as the fundamental flavors in masala chai. If you have masala tea, you can simply use it and omit the whole spices. Add more or less sugar than called for here to suit your preference for sweetness.

TIME
Total Time: about 2 hours
Active Time: 15 minutes

INGREDIENTS
4 cups (1 litre) water
1/2 - 3/4 cup (100-150 grams) granulated sugar
6 black tea bags (or 2 tablespoons black tea leaves)
3 whole cloves
1 cinnamon stick
1 star anise
1 cardamom pod
Ice
About 1 cup (240 mL) heavy cream, half and half, or coconut milk
2 teaspoons vanilla extract (optional)

PREPARATION

1. Brew the tea: In a medium pot, bring the water to a boil. Add the sugar and stir until the sugar dissolves, then turn off the heat and add the tea, cloves, cinnamon, star anise, and cardamom. Let the tea steep for 20-30 minutes—it should be very strong.

2. Chill: Pour the tea through a fine mesh strainer to remove the tea and spices. Let the tea cool to room temperature, then put it in the fridge to cool completely.

3. Mix: Place a generous handful of ice cubes in 4-6 tall glasses. Pour the tea over, filling the glasses about ¾ full. Add cream or half and half to fill each glass, then add a dash of vanilla extract. Stir gently to combine. Taste; add tea, cream, or sugar to your liking, then serve.

NOTES

Feel free to play around with the sweetness of this recipe. Instead of sweetening the tea itself, for example, you can use sweetened condensed milk, which lets you adjust the tea's sweetness upon serving (see page 246 for a homemade sweetened condensed milk recipe). Or, you can sweeten it using a masala-infused simple syrup, like Marula Mercantile's (see page 257).

Taste of Jamaica

Sophia Jones is both a first and second generation immigrant, and has a keen understanding of what it's like to straddle cultures and identities. Born in a London suburb to Jamaican parents, she grew up immersed in Jamaican culture. Her parents immigrated in the 1950s as a part of the Windrush era, when the UK opened its doors to mass immigration from the Commonwealth. Most immigrants came from rural backgrounds, and many, like her father, were descendents of people who fought in WWII. Her mother worked as a nurse and her father in a factory, and they clung to their Jamaican culture despite living in a predominantly white community. Never letting go of their roots, Sophia's family visited Jamaica frequently, and her parents eventually retired there.

Church played a significant role in her family life, and from childhood, Sophia was an active member of the choir. Her church had an exchange program with a Kenyan church, and she became so infatuated with Kenyan culture that she recounts the time when, at eight years old, her friend Stephen teased that someday she'd go to Kenya and marry a Kenyan. Sure enough, when she turned eighteen, she traveled to Kenya for the first time. She describes that experience as a "homecoming" and she knew that she was "going to end up here." She spent six months in Thika working in a school, and it was during this time that she met her future husband. They kept in touch after she returned to the UK for university. She returned to Nairobi after graduation and they married. She laughingly recalls how, at her wedding, her mother pulled a bottle of hot sauce out of her handbag during the meal: always Jamaican, even in Africa.

Sophia and her husband lived between the UK and Kenya, and she built a career in communications, working for NGOs. They eventually separated, but she remained in Kenya.

Sophia had always dreamed of opening a restaurant, and when her contract ended with the NGO she'd been working for in Nairobi, she decided that it was time to take the leap. She traveled to Gambia for two weeks on a research trip, where she worked in a Jamaican friend's restaurant to learn the ropes. She brought her cousin from Jamaica to be the chef, and in the fall of 2015, Taste of Jamaica opened to the public. Sophia describes the restaurant as a place for food, but also a place to learn about Jamaican culture. Inside, the walls are painted light yellow, and each room has a theme. There's the Usain Bolt room, though Sophia quickly points out photos of accomplished female track stars that hang next to glamour shots of Jamaica's most famous athlete. There's the reggae room with posters of famous bands and musicians, including, of course, Bob Marley. On Sundays, the restaurant hosts daytime reggae concerts, featuring Kenyan reggae bands, and Sophie noted that they'd like the restaurant to become a hub for up-and-coming artists.

Kenya has a long history of Caribbean immigration. The organist at Sophia's wedding was from Trinidad, and Jamaica was one of the founding members of UNEP, which has headquarters in Nairobi. Nairobi's first Jamaican restaurant, Taste of Jamaica reflects this history in its own name: a beautiful, delicious taste of Sophia's beloved culture, food and history.

s̃

NOTE: Taste of Jamaica closed at the end of June 2016.

Afghan House

It all started with the baklava--perfectly crispy, perfectly sweet and perfectly delicious. When Mehnaz Sarwar and her husband Abu-Bakr decided to start an Afghan food business in 2013, they started with baklava. Abu-Bakr came from a long line of bakers, his family owns the famous Azizi Bakery in Kabul, and he grew up making sweets. They wanted to make all types if Afghan food, but baklava was the one that sold the best. Even the baklava took multiple iterations, though. When they started, Abu-Bakr made Afghani-style baklava, which has a thick, fluffy pastry dough. They realized that their customers were more accustomed to Turkish-style baklava that's lighter and crispy from the very thin filo, so they adapted. Abu-Bakr makes the filo fresh daily by hand, and they made deliveries all over Nairobi.

Before they realized the market for baklava, they unsuccessfully tried selling prepared food at their mosque after Friday prayers. The venture failed, and they ended up taking the food home and sharing with their family and friends. Facebook created an opportunity for them to reach out to a broader range of customers and establish their credibility. Because of the large expat community in Nairobi, there are Facebook groups dedicated to various interests and needs of people far away from home looking for help or community. Mehnaz realized the opportunity to advertise to a captive audience, and started posting about her food. The first time she posted, so many orders came in that she jumped in to help her husband cook, baby in tow. Soon they'd built such a large and loyal customer base that they started doing pop-up restaurants around town, and in July 2016, they opened their own restaurant, Afghan House.

In some ways their story seems like an overnight success, but the journey that brought them to where they are now reflects a larger, global story of migration. Mehnaz was born and raised in Kenya in a prosperous family that emigrated from South Asia, today's Pakistan, five generations ago. She went to the UK for university, studying travel and tourism, and her family eventually joined her there. She stayed after graduating and worked in marketing, and met her future husband, Abu-Bakr, who'd emigrated from Afghanistan and was working in construction. They married in 2009 and moved to Kabul to be closer to his family and also to escape the discrimination she faced daily as a Muslim woman who veiled in the UK. Mehnaz wears a niqab and is careful to state that she made the decision to veil when she turned twenty years old, and she's proud of her choices. She hoped to find more acceptance and safety in Kabul, but still found herself unhappy. After two years, she and her husband decided to move in with her family in Nairobi. Now they live in the family home, a large estate with separate apartments for everyone. She now has the freedom she'd sought elsewhere to live as she'd like and be left alone. People simply don't care, she exclaimed with satisfaction.

Today she and her husband are focused on expanding their menu of Afghan classics and raising their three young children. It's a family business, with Abu-Bakr in the kitchen making the food he grew up with, Mehnaz taking orders and the children running all over the place. Theirs is a quintessentially modern story, enabled by technology, supported by a global community, and appreciated by all.

TASTE OF JAMAICA

GUINNESS PUNCH

MAKES
One tall glass of punch

Sophia explains that the Guinness punch of her childhood was made with Nutrament, a Nestlé nutritional supplement popular in Jamaica in the 1980s and 90s. We find that a mix of whole milk and sweetened condensed milk does the trick, though you can always go a step further and throw some vanilla ice cream in the mix.

TIME
Total Time: 5 minutes
Active Time: 5 minutes

INGREDIENTS
6 ounces (170 mL) very cold Guinness
1/2 cup (120 mL) whole milk
2 tablespoons sweetened condensed milk
Pinch of nutmeg
Water, optional
Ice

PREPARATION
1. Combine the Guinness, milk, and sweetened condensed milk in a tall glass. Stir to combine, then add a handful of ice cubes. (If you'd like a milder version of the punch, add water little by little to your liking.) Top with a pinch of nutmeg and serve.

NOTES
If you don't have sweetened condensed milk, you can easily make your own. Simply combine 1 cup (240 mL) milk with 1/3 cup (65 grams) sugar in a small saucepan. Bring the milk to a boil, then reduce the heat to low and simmer, whisking constantly, for about 20 minutes, until the volume of the milk has reduced to under 1/2 cup. Let the sweetened condensed milk cool to room temperature and then refrigerate before using it in your punch.

─── MARULA MERCANTILE ───

CAPE FEAR PUNCH

SERVES
About 6

This cocktail playfully reinterprets Kenyan chai tea, which is heavy with flavors of cardamom, cinnamon, and black pepper. Unlike Kenyan chai, this cocktail is not overly sweet. You will have simple syrup left over if you make the full amount; divide it by four if you really don't want leftovers (though, believe us, this will become your simple syrup recipe of choice).

TIME
Total Time: 4 hours
Active Time: 20 minutes

INGREDIENTS FOR THE COCKTAIL

Peel of 1 whole orange
Peel of 1 whole lemon
1/4 cup (50 grams) granulated sugar
1/4 cup (60 mL) brewed black tea, chilled
1/4 cup (60 mL) chai simple syrup (see below)
1 1/2 cups + 1 tablespoon (375 mL) bourbon
2 cups (480 mL) sugar-free orange juice, cold
1/4 cup (60 mL) fresh lime juice
About 1 1/2 cups (360 mL) soda water, to taste
Ice

FOR THE CHAI SIMPLE SYRUP

1 cup (200 grams) granulated sugar
1 cup (240 mL) water
1 teaspoon ground cinnamon
1 teaspoon ground black pepper
1 teaspoon ground cardamom
1 teaspoon nutmeg

PREPARATION

1. Make the citrus sugar: Use a sharp knife or a vegetable peeler to remove the orange and lemon peels in thin strips. Place the peels in a small bowl and sprinkle the 1/4 cup of granulated sugar over. Use your fingers to rub the sugar into the peels, then let the mixture sit for at least three hours (or overnight, in the fridge).

2. Make the chai syrup: Combine the cup of granulated sugar, water, cinnamon, black pepper, cardamom, and nutmeg in a small saucepan. Simmer, stirring, until the sugar dissolves into the water. Let the simple syrup cool to room temperature, then put it in the fridge to chill.

3. Brew the black tea: Boil a cup of water and steep a tea bag of black tea for 8-10 minutes. Remove the tea bag and cool the tea to room temperature, then let it chill in the fridge.

4. Mix: Combine the bourbon, orange juice, lime juice, and black tea in a large pitcher or punch bowl. Stir in 1/4 cup (60 mL) of the chai simple syrup, all the citrus sugar (along with the citrus peels), ice, and soda water. Stir well, then taste; add extra chai syrup until it's as sweet as you like it.

5. Serve: Serve in punch glasses, with a strip of lemon & orange peel in each one.

NOTES

If the sediment in the simple syrup bothers you, you can strain the cooled simple syrup through a cheesecloth before using it.

CHEKA

CHUHAI (GRAPEFRUIT COCKTAIL)

SERVES
1

This mild, pleasantly tart cocktail is a perfect weekday drink. For more of a kick, up the ratio of soju to your liking. To make drinks for a crowd, multiply the recipe as needed.

TIME
Total Time: 5 minutes
Active Time: 5 minutes

PREPARATION
1. In a medium tumbler, muddle the honey with the grapefruit juice. Add the soju and stir to combine. Add a couple of ice cubes and top off with soda water.
2. Taste; adjust to your liking.

INGREDIENTS
1 teaspoon honey
1/8 cup (30 mL) fresh grapefruit juice
1/8 cup (30 mL) Japanese soju
1/2 cup (120 mL) soda water
Ice

 JUNIPER SOCIAL

GIN DAWA

 SERVES
1

Meaning *medicine* in Swahili, the dawa is a simple, delicious cocktail with just four ingredients. The Juniper Social puts its own spin on the classic drink by using gin instead of the more traditional vodka. The key to a perfect dawa? Use room temperature gin. This allows the honey to dissolve quickly and completely in the alcohol.

 TIME
Total Time: 5 minutes
Active Time: 5 minutes

INGREDIENTS
3 tablespoons (45ml) gin (Juniper prefers Beefeater)
1 1/2 teaspoons honey
1 fresh lime, cut into six wedges, seeds removed
Generous handful of crushed ice

 PREPARATION

1. Muddle: Pour 45ml of gin into a tumbler. Add the honey and stir until it dissolves. Add 4 lime wedges to the glass and muddle with a spoon.

2. Finish: Add crushed ice to fill the glass and stir everything together. Let the dawa sit for at least 5 minutes before serving; the melting ice dilutes the gin just enough to make a perfectly drinkable cocktail. Garnish with 2 lime wedges on the rim of the glass.

NOTES
Don't have fancy crushed ice on hand? No problem. Wrap a handful of ice cubes in a clean kitchen towel, gather up the corners, and hit the bundle against a counter or floor a couple of times. Voilà: crushed ice!

~~ JUNIPER SOCIAL ~~

GIN BASIL FIZZ

 SERVES
1

This cocktail begs to be served at a picnic or garden party. If you prefer your drinks a bit less sweet, replace half the tonic with soda water. To scale it up, multiply the recipe as needed and serve it out of a big pitcher.

 PREPARATION

1. Put the cucumber and basil leaves into a large tumbler.
2. Add the ice, gin, and tonic. Stir gently. Taste; adjust as desired.

TIME
Total Time: 5 minutes
Active Time: 5 minutes

 INGREDIENTS

3 tablespoons (45mL) gin (Beefeater or Hendricks)
2 thin slices of cucumber
3 basil leaves
2/3 cup (160 mL) tonic
Handful of ice cubes

Som Tam Thai

I've always been one of those who scours blogs, newspapers and magazines for info on new restaurants, and in Nairobi I pride myself on being "in the know." I was totally blindsided by Som Tam Thai. I've long lamented the lack of Southeast Asian restaurants in the city, and when one finally opens, I don't find out until three months later!

In some ways, it's understandable (making excuses for myself here). This tiny restaurant inhabits one and a half rooms, enough for six tables with four chairs apiece and a kitchen about the size of one of the tables, downstairs from one of Nairobi's most notorious nightclubs. The building itself is nondescript; few seem to go there in the daytime. There's a shop selling clothes with eerily human-looking mannequins standing at the entrance of the building, across is a fast-food joint selling fried chicken to-go, and there's a shop with shoes piled from floor to ceiling. Nestled in between is this jewel of a restaurant, painted blinding bright pink and blue with the most amazing smells of citrus and fish sauce wafting out the door. It's as if a street stall were airlifted from Bangkok and dropped into the building in the heart of Electric Avenue.

The tables are covered in doilies, which are covered in plastic. Food comes out on small plastic plates covered in Christmas patterns and random Americana. No plate is the same, and it's oddly fitting to be served a tear-inducing papaya salad on a teddy bear plate. In Thai, som tam translates into papaya salad. It's impossible to eat here without ordering their namesake dish, it's aggressively sweet, spicy, tart and crunchy, memorable and tongue-searing.

Kwanduban Punlee moved to Nairobi a year ago to work as a bakery consultant for a high-end local restaurant chain. She'd been a baking instructor in Bangkok for twelve years, so it was a straightforward transition. After six months, she left to become the head chef at a Thai restaurant in Village Market, a shopping center near the United Nations. The owner there was Kenyan Indian and the staff had never worked under a Thai chef before. Omar, a cook at SomTam Thai, first met Mrs. Punlee at this restaurant. He fell in love with her cooking, and when she opened SomTam Thai in early 2016, he followed her to this new venture. He refers to her as "mama," a traditional honorific, and exclaims, "She taught us real Thai food!"

Mrs. Punlee owns the restaurant with her husband, though he is based in Bangkok, traveling back and forth to Nairobi. He is a former bodyguard of the Thai princess, and started coming to Nairobi recently to import food products. Kenya is the only country that Mrs. Punlee has visited outside of Thailand, and she's committing to staying long term. Two months after opening, her brother and sister joined her here. Neither she nor her sister has children, and her brother has two, who remain in Bangkok.

It's interesting to think about how different cuisines can be, even with access to the same ingredients. Mrs. Punlee can get nearly all the ingredients that she needs locally for the restaurant, and yet her food couldn't be more different from most other food in the city. Though she and her family may be soft-spoken, their food shouts aggressively, bringing those in the know back for more.

~ MARULA MERCANTILE ~

BLOODY MARY

 **SERVES**
4

Marula Mercantile's Bloody Mary is not for the faint of heart. It is boldly spicy, salty, and tomatoey in the best way.

 TIME
Total Time: 10 minutes
Active Time: 10 minutes

 INGREDIENTS FOR THE COCKTAIL

3 cups (about 450 grams) cherry tomatoes, plus a few extra to garnish
2 tablespoons grated horseradish
1 tablespoon hot sauce
1/2 tablespoon Worcestershire sauce
1 teaspoon celery salt
1 tablespoon salt
1 tablespoon fresh lime juice
A few grinds of black pepper
3/4 cup (180 mL) vodka
4 cornichons, to garnish
Ice

 PREPARATION

1. Make the Bloody Mary mix: Put the cherry tomatoes in a blender and blend them thoroughly. Add the horseradish, hot sauce, Worcestershire sauce, celery salt, salt, lime juice, and black pepper. Blend until the mixture is homogenous. Taste; add more salt, chili, and lime to your liking.

2. Spike: In a tall glass, combine ½ cup (120 mL) of the mix with 3 tablespoons vodka. Add plenty of ice and stir. Taste; add vodka if you'd like your drink a bit stronger. Repeat with the remaining glasses.

3. Garnish: Serve the drinks with a skewer or stirring stick topped off with a cornichon and a cherry tomato.

NOTES

If you can't find celery salt, you can easily make your own. Simply trim the leaves from a bunch of celery, clean them, and spread them evenly on a baking tray. Bake in an oven heated to 350F (175C) for 5-7 minutes, until the leaves are very dry but not browned. Let them cool, then crumble them with your fingers. Combine the crumbled leaves with flaky sea salt in equal quantities: 2 tablespoons dried celery to 2 tablespoons salt, for example. Store the salt in a jar and keep it on hand for Bloody Marys, or to sprinkle on soup, grilled corn, or potatoes.

MARULA MERCANTILE

CAPE FEAR PUNCH

SERVES
6

This cocktail playfully reinterprets Kenyan chai tea, which is heavy with flavors of cardamom, cinnamon, and black pepper. Unlike Kenyan chai, this cocktail is not made overly sweet. You will have simple syrup left over if you make the full amount; divide it by four if you really don't want leftovers (though, believe us, this will become your simple syrup recipe of choice).

TIME
Total Time: 3 hours
Active Time: 20 minutes

PREPARATION

1. Make the citrus sugar: Use a sharp knife or a vegetable peeler to remove the orange and lemon peels in thin strips. Place the peels in a small bowl and sprinkle the ¼ cup of granulated sugar over. Use your fingers to rub the sugar into the peels, then let the mixture sit for at least three hours (or overnight, in the fridge).

INGREDIENTS FOR THE COCKTAIL

Peel of 1 whole orange
Peel of 1 whole lemon
¼ cup (50 grams) granulated sugar
¼ cup (60 mL) brewed black tea, chilled
¼ cup (60 mL) chai simple syrup (recipe to follow)
1 ½ cups + 1 tablespoon (375 mL) bourbon
2 cups (475 mL) sugar-free orange juice, cold
¼ cup (60 mL) fresh lime juice
About 1 ½ cups (360 mL) soda water, to taste
ice

2. Make the chai syrup: Combine the cup of granulated sugar, water, cinnamon, black pepper, cardamom, and nutmeg in a small saucepan. Simmer, stirring, until the sugar dissolves into the water. Let the simple syrup cool to room temperature, then put it in the fridge to chill.

3. Brew the black tea: Boil a cup of water and steep a teabag of black tea for 8-10 minutes. Remove the teabag and let the tea cool to room temperature, then let it chill in the fridge.

4. Mix: Combine the bourbon, orange juice, lime juice, and black tea in a large pitcher or punch bowl. Stir in ¼ cup (60 mL) of the chai simple syrup, all the citrus sugar (along with the citrus peels), ice, and soda water. Taste; add extra chai syrup until it's as sweet as you like it.

5. Serve: Serve in punch glasses, with a strip of lemon & orange peel in each one.

INGREDIENTS FOR THE CHAI SIMPLE SYRUP

1 cup (200 grams) granulated sugar
1 cup (240 mL) water
1 teaspoon ground cinnamon
1 teaspoon ground black pepper
1 teaspoon ground cardamom
1 teaspoon nutmeg

Reference Charts

WEIGHT

US	Metric
½ ounce	15 grams
1 ounce	30 grams
2 ounces	60 grams
¼ pound	115 grams
1/3 pound	150 grams
½ pound	225 grams
¾ pound	350 grams
1 pound	450 grams

TEMPERATURE

Fahrenheit	Celsius
250°F	120°C
275°F	135°C
300°F	150°C
325°F	160°C
350°F	175°C
375°F	190°C
400°F	200°C
425°F	220°C
450°F	245°C

LIQUID VOLUME

U.S	Imperial	Metric
1 teaspoon	--	5 mL
1 tablespoon	½ fluid ounce	15 mL
2 tablespoons	1 fluid ounce	30 mL
¼ cup	2 fluid ounces	60 mL
1/3 cup	3 fluid ounces	90 mL
½ cup	4 fluid ounces	120 mL
1 cup	8 fluid ounces	240 mL
4 cups	32 fluid ounces	1 litre

Index

Abyssinia
242 Tri-Level Juice

Afghan
Afghan House
154 Scallion Dumplings
188 Mutton Shorva

62 *Al Yusra*
106 Daillo,
82 Pasta Saldato,
 Somali Rice,

American
132 *Marula Mercantile*
256 Biscuit Sammy,
257 Bloody Mary,
64 Cape Fear Punch,
 Plum Pecorino Salad,

Australian
Juniper Social
122 Asian Slaw,
250 Gin Basil Fizz,
248 Gin Dawa,

Beans
184 Feijoada
196 Bean Stew with Plantains,
30 Fuul,

Beef
58 Beef Noodle Soup
164 Beef Burger,
74 La Tagliata,
170 Meat Patties,
150 Pytt-i-Panna,
154 Scallion Dumplings
176 Steak Skewers

Belle Ambiance
148 Duck Confit,
220 Galette des Rois,

Bodyzone
54 Okra Stew
212 Sauce Poisson
210 Samaki Moshi

Bok choi
58 Beef Noodle Soup,
140 Hot pot,
142 Shui Zhu Pork,

100 Yaki Udon

Brazilian
Churrasco Gaucho
226 Crème Caramel
86 Farofa,
184 Feijoada,
192 Moqueca of Prawns,
176 Steak Skewers,

British
Purdy Arms
164 Beef Burger,
166 Caramelized Onions,
234 Chocolate Marshmallow Samosas,
63 Apple Coleslaw,
18 Tomato Brie Samosas,

Cai Lan Chao Shi
58 Beef Noodle Soup,
26 Fried Pork Dumplings,
28 Seafood Wontons,

Cake
222 Black Cake,
228 Vanilla Chai Cake,
236 Matcha Green Tea Cake

Cedars
10 Baba Ghanoush,
14 Labneh,
12 Pickles,

Cheese
22 Mozzarella,
106 Pasta Saldato,
156 Pizza,
64 Plum & Pecorino Salad,
126 Ravioli with Spinach & Ricotta,
18 Tomato & Brie Samosas

Cheka
44 Braised Pork Belly,
172 Chicken Teriyaki
46 Fried Octopus,
247 Chuhai,

Chengdu Impressions
162 Hui Gou Rou (Twice Cooked Pork),
108 Mapo Tofu,
142 Shui Zhu Pork,

Chicken
146 Murg Makhani,
172 Chicken Teriyaki,
40 Chicken Wings,
136 Jerk Chicken,
150 Pytt-i-Panna,

Chinese
Cai Lan Chao Shi
58 Beef Noodle Soup,
26 Fried Pork Dumplings,
28 Seafood Wontons,
Chengdu Impressions
162 Hui Gou Rou (Twice Cooked Pork),
108 Mapo Tofu,
142 Shui Zhu Pork,
Tin Tin
40 Chicken Wings,
56 Wintermelon Soup

Chocolate
234 Chocolate Marshmallow Samosas,

Chowpaty
128 Garlic Butter Masala Dosa,
118 Paneer Tikka Masala
90 Special Garlic Chips

Churrasco Gaucho
226 Crème Caramel
86 Farofa,
184 Feijoada,
192 Moqueca of Prawns,
176 Steak Skewers,

Congolese
Bodyzone,
54 Okra Stew
212 Sauce Poisson
210 Samaki Moshi

Crab
214 Crab & Ginger Pasta,
208 Seafood Marmite,

D'Afric
120 Falafel,
30 Fuul,
32 Salata Aswat,

Duck
148 Duck Confit with Gratin Potatoes,

259

Index

Eggplant
- 10 Baba Ghanoush,
- 32 Salata Aswat,
- 100 Yaki Udon,

Ethiopian
Abyssinia
- 242 Tri-Level Juice

*Habesha
- 110 Injera
- 112 Shiro Wat
- 113 Spicy Lentils
- 114 Vegetable Platter

Fish
- 200 Grilled Salmon,
- 212 Sauce Poisson,
- 210 Samaki Moshi,
- 208 Seafood Marmite,

French
Belle Ambiance
- 148 Duck Confit with Gratin Potatoes,
- 220 Galette des Rois

Table 49
- 208 Seafood Marmite

Furusato
- 194 Caterpillar Sushi,
- 36 Tempura Prawns,

Goat
- 62 Daillo
- 188 Mutton Shorva

Han Di Yuan
- 70 Cucumber Cold Dish,
- 96 Kimchi Fried Rice,

Hot Pot
- 140 Hot Pot

Indian
Chowpaty
- 128 Garlic Butter Masala Dosa
- 118 Paneer Tikka Masala
- 90 Special Garlic Chips

Open House
- 38 Chilly Garlic Mushroom
- 146 Murg Makhani

Italian
Osteria
- 20 Pesto
- 156 Pizzas
- 22 Mozzarella

Trattoria
- 214 Crab & Ginger Pasta
- 182 Pasta Carbonara

La Salumeria
- 74 La Tagliata
- 126 Ravioli with Spinach and Ricotta

Jamaican
Taste of Jamaica
- 222 Black Cake,
- 246 Guinness Punch,
- 136 Jerk Chicken,
- 170 Meat Patties,
- 94 Rice and Peas,

Japanese
Cheka
- 44 Braised Pork Belly,
- 172 Chicken Teriyaki,
- 46 Fried Octopus,
- 247 Chuhai

Misono
- 102 Avocado Uramaki,
- 200 Grilled Salmon,
- 100 Yaki Udon,

Furusato
- 194 Caterpillar Sushi,
- 36 Tempura Prawns,

Sushi Soo
- 180 Pork Katsudon,
- 202 Dynamite Futo Maki Roll,
- 236 Matcha Green Tea Cake

Juniper Social
- 122 Asian Slaw,
- 250 Gin Basil Fizz,
- 248 Gin Dawa,

La Salumeria
- 74 La Tagliata,
- 126 Ravioli with Spinach and Ricotta,

Lebanese
Cedars
- 10 Baba Ghanoush,
- 14 Labneh,
- 12 Pickles,

Mama Ashanti
- 190 Bean Stew with Plantains,
- 88 Jollof Rice
- 72 Nigerian Pepper Soup

Marula Mercantile
- 132 Biscuit Sammy,
- 256 Bloody Mary,
- 257 Cape Fear Punch,
- 64 Plum Pecorino Salad,

Misono
- 102 Avocado Uramaki,
- 200 Grilled Salmon,
- 100 Yaki Udon,

Moniko's
- 230 Apple Crisp,
- 150 Pytt-i-Panna,
- 78 Spicy Calamari Salad,

Mushroom
- 38 Chilly Garlic Mushroom,
- 70 Cucumber Cold Dish,
- 140 Hot Pot,
- 50 Tom Yam Kung

Nigerian
Mama Ashanti
- 190 Bean Stew with Plantains,
- 88 Jollof Rice,
- 72 Nigerian Pepper Soup,

Noodles
- 58 Beef Noodle Soup,
- 100 Yaki Udon,

Open House
- 38 Chilly Garlic Mushroom
- 146 Murg Makhani

Osteria
- 20 Pesto
- 156 Pizzas
- 22 Mozzarella

Paneer
- 118 Paneer Tikka Masala,

Pasta
- 214 Crab & Ginger Pasta,
- 182 Pasta Carbonara,
- 106 Pasta Saldato,

Index

126   Ravioli with Spinach and Ricotta,

Pork
- 132   Biscuit Sammy,
- 44   Braised Pork Belly,
- 184   Feijoada,
- 162   Hui Gou Rou (Twice Cooked Pork),
- 26   Fried Pork Dumplings,
- 180   Pork Katsudon,
- 28   Seafood Wontons,

Potato
- 148   Duck Confit with Gratin Potatoes,
- 128   Garlic Butter Masala Dosa,
- 150   Pytt-i-Panna
- 90   Special Garlic Chips,
- 114   Ethiopian Vegetable Platter,

Prawns
- 208   Seafood Marmite
- 36   Tempura Prawns
- 50   Tom Yam Kung

Purdy Arms
- 63   Apple Coleslaw,
- 164   Beef Burger,
- 166   Caramelized Onions,
- 234   Chocolate Marshmallow Samosas,
- 18   Tomato Brie Samosas,

Rice
- 88   Jollof Rice,
- 96   Kimchi Fried Rice,
- 94   Rice and Peas,
- 82   Somali Rice,

Somali
Al Yusra
- 62   Daillo,
- 106   Pasta Saldato,
- 82   Somali Rice,

Sudanese
D'Afric
- 120   Falafel,
- 30   Fuul,
- 32   Salata Aswat,

Sushi

- 102   Avocado Uramaki,
- 194   Caterpillar Sushi,
- 202   Dynamite Fuko Maki,

Sushi Soo
- 182   Pork Katsudon,
- 202   Dynamite Futo Maki Roll,
- 236   Matcha Green Tea Cake,

Swedish
Moniko's
- 230   Apple Crisp,
- 150   Pytt-i-Panna,
- 78   Spicy Calamari Salad,

Table 49
- 208   Seafood Marmite,

Taste of Jamaica
- 222   Black Cake,
- 246   Guinness Punch,
- 136   Jerk Chicken,
- 170   Meat Patties,
- 94   Rice and Peas,

Thai
Som Tam Thai
- 66   Som Tam (Green Papaya Salad),
- 50   Tom Yam Kung (Sweet & Sour Soup),

Tin Tin
- 40   Chicken Wings,
- 56   Melon Soup,

Tofu
- 122   Asian Slaw,
- 70   Cucumber Cold Dish,
- 140   Hot Pot,
- 108   Mapo Tofu,

Tomato
- 192   Moqueca Prawns,
- 54   Okra Stew
- 118   Paneer Tikka Masala,
- 106   Pasta Saldato,
- 212   Sauce Poisson,
- 18   Tomato & Brie Samosas,

Trattoria
- 182   Pasta Carbonara
- 214   Crab & Ginger Pasta

Acknowledgments

Huge thanks to all of our wonderful Kickstarter supporters:

Ariel Zirulnick, Sophie Kainen, Eduardo Montero, Gabrielle Cornish, Kirtley Righi, Jen Card, Addison Steele, Kevin Koplan, Kevin Rosenberg, Nancy & Terry Robrecht, Alicia Sully, Tammy Guo, Cayla Marvil, Hannah Postel, Connor Wakayama, Adam & Erin Rokey-Strom, Jesse Elizabeth Dean, Jerry Zhao, Meagan, Elisabeth Seite, Devin MacDonald, Kimberly Behrman, Alice E. Pang, Jay Taneja & Emily Kumpel, Elizabeth Resor, Kristen Ann Tymeson, Kerry Diamond & Claudia Wu, Krissy Glauser, Michelle Malecki, Matt Groh, Patricia Murphy,
Eric Elderbrock, Charlie Ackerly, Sarah Lusche, Bob Myers & Sakiko Kimura, Zeena A Wilson, Mir Bear-Johnson, Rishan Chandarana, Ana Cristina Garcia, Ori Pleban, Jenel Cohen, David Yoon, Tyler Tate, Brandon Vaughan, Hunter Tanous, Charlotte & Francesco, R. Gothie, Sondre Nilsen, Ryan Handberg, JJ Sommerville, Kieran J. Wilkie, Justin Bahn, Charlie Hofmann, Elizabeth O'Grady, The Thompson Family (Phoenix, AZ), Hannah Stork, Jenn Cotter, Angelo Fu, Dorothy Lyman, Ash Dysart Miller, Piermur, Jade Thomson, Katy Hill, Graeme Henson, Andreas Michael, Tim Rodriguez, Adam Luptak, Erin Foster, Anna Flinchbaugh, Jeannie Bartlett, Sarah Doherty, Jaewon Oh, Wendy Brooke Jenkins, Angela Santee, Jeremy Gordon, Annie Roberts, Kevin Miles Irby, Chris Opila, Ana Margarita Paz, Cathy Nunnally & Lex Gillan, Kelly DeHay, Christina & Mike Elliott, Joshua Smith,
Bernardo van de Schepop, Ronald & Linda, Cees de Groot, Carole Zoom, Matthew Hardin, Miriam Nielsen, Elaine M. Cassell, Jane Yang, Mark & Kim,
JP Rangaswami, Ann Craven, Spencer Nageleisen, Geneviève Grand, Cynthia Ryan, The Reis Family, Danielle Rougeau, Catherine Boyer & Peter Lusche, Laurin & Alyssa Dodd, Charles & Ellen Cooreman